EUROCOMMUNISM

EUROCOMMUNISM

BY STEPHEN GOODE

Franklin Watts
New York | London | Toronto | Sydney | 1980
An Impact Book

Photographs courtesy of:
United Press International:
pp. 6, 31, 42, 45, 54, 63, 78, 94;
The New York Public Library
Picture Collection: pp. 13, 16.

Library of Congress Cataloging in Publication Data

Goode, Stephen.
Eurocommunism.

(An Impact book)
Includes index.
SUMMARY: Explains what Eurocommunism is, traces
its history, and presents an overview of its existence
in Italy, France, and Spain where its doctrines have
grown in strength in recent years.
1. Communism—Europe—Juvenile literature. 2. Communism—History—Juvenile literature. [1. Communism—Europe. 2. Communism—History] I. Title.
HX238.5.G66   335.43'094   79-26225
ISBN 0-531-02857-7

HX238
.5
.G66

CONTENTS

CHAPTER ONE

WHAT IS EUROCOMMUNISM?

One of the most significant and widely discussed political events of recent years has been the growing strength of communism in Italy, France, and Spain. Once regarded with mistrust—if not open hostility—the Communists have acquired a new respectability and popularity. Sizable numbers of Italian, French, and Spanish voters regularly support Communist candidates for public office. In the future, it is possible that Communists will hold Cabinet-level posts and share national power with other political parties. What many experts believed impossible only a few years ago—the full participation by the Communist parties of Western Europe in all aspects of government—now seems to be a near reality.

Several reasons help explain this change in public attitude. Some observers trace the change to a lessening of Cold War tensions which has made communism appear less menacing. The antagonisms of an earlier generation—when the

Soviet Union and the West stood on the brink of war—have been replaced by feelings of mutual acceptance and toleration, at least among a significant number of people.

Other observers find the reason for the new popularity of communism in the prolonged economic crisis Europe has been experiencing since the early 1970s. According to this view, rising unemployment and high rates of inflation have led to voter dissatisfaction with the political parties in power and this dissatisfaction, in turn, has led to protest at the polls. Angered by the failure to find work or by an inability to make ends meet, the people of France, Italy, and Spain have cast their ballots in increasing numbers for Communist candidates in order to register their complaints and objections with the *status quo* and demand that steps be taken to improve the economic situation.

But perhaps the most important factor in the growing popularity of communism has been the removal, by some of the Communists themselves, of many of the more objectionable elements from Communist doctrine—its rigidity, its inclination toward totalitarianism, its intolerance of other ideas—and the replacement of these elements with a new commitment to the democratic system and to individual liberty. As a result, the old fear that communism cares nothing for democracy or freedom has been largely defused. Communism has gained respectability and prestige because it has begun to speak a new language, a language that respects civil rights and private property and a language that has abandoned dictatorship and violent revolution.

In 1975, this new form of communism was dubbed Eurocommunism by an Italian journalist who wanted to distinguish it from the forms of communism practiced in the Soviet Union, Eastern Europe, China, and elsewhere.

The Eurocommunists claim to remain loyal to the political philosophy of Karl Marx and Friedrich Engels, the founders of modern communism. Like other Communists they seek to end economic exploitation and hope to establish economic, social, and political equality for all men and women. They hope to upset the power of big business, industry, and the great banks and to distribute the wealth of society among all its citizens.

Where Eurocommunism differs from other forms of communism is on the means to attain these ends. Since 1917, when violent revolution led to the establishment of communism in Russia, Communist theorists in the Soviet Union have tended to regard their revolution as the model for all Communist revolutions. At some point in the change from capitalism to communism, they believe, force and violence will probably have to be used in order to destroy the past, root out the old order, and make way for a new social and economic system.

The Eurocommunists, on the other hand, claim they no longer hold this belief. They argue that the aims of communism can be achieved by peaceful means, through participation in the democratic system and the use of the ballot box. They say they prefer a gradual transformation of society from capitalism to communism to the abrupt change and extreme disruption caused by revolution.

The leading figures of the Spanish, Italian, and French Communist parties have defended the doctrines of Eurocommunism for the past ten years in numerous books, articles, and speeches. Santiago Carrillo, head of the Spanish Communist party (PCE) and one of the leading architects of Eurocommunism, has promised that his party will pay "full respect" to free elections and will contribute all it can to the development of freedom and individual liberty in Spain. The international Communist movement, he says, is not a Church with dogmas that must be believed and practiced by every Communist. Communism can vary from country to country. Where democracy thrives, communism can become democratic.

In his book *Eurocommunism and the State,* Carrillo has presented a thorough exposition of his ideas. The chief problem with communism in the Soviet Union and Eastern Europe, he writes, is that it has never solved the problem of "democratization." Inequalities still exist in those countries, yet a "unilateral propaganda machine" forbids all open discussion. The mission of Eurocommunism, he says, is to prove that communism can work in Western Europe without it being an extension of Soviet power and without the "one-party" Soviet system that destroys freedom. Eurocommunism must be "an independent experience with a more advanced socialism that will have a positive influence on the democratic evolution [of the societies that exist today]."

In Italy—where the Communist party enjoys widespread support and a large membership—the ideas of Eurocommunism are defended by the highly respected party chief, Enrico Berlinguer. On numerous occasions, Berlinguer has said that Italian Communists see no need for violent revolution or Communist dictatorship in Italy. Indeed, he claims, the Communists want to preserve Italy's "pluralist" society, a society where men and women of a variety of beliefs can live comfortably and securely, side by side. The example of the Soviet Union, he concludes, holds no promise for the peoples of the West, where different conditions and orientations demand different solutions to political and social problems.

Similar views are expressed by Georges Marchais, the leader of the well-organized and influential French Communist party (PCF). In his book *The Democratic Challenge,* which represents not only his own beliefs but the position of his party as well, Marchais insists that French communism offers no danger to the democratic process and is dedicated to the rule of law, the parliamentary system, and the French way of life. The Communist party, he argues, works for the benefit of all French people—the middle class as well as the working class, Christians as well as nonbelievers.

In 1976, in a speech before the 22nd Conference of the PCF, Marchais declared, "Our road to communism is an original road . . . a French road." What the party seeks, he added, is a "diversity that enriches . . . [not a] garrison communism that casts everyone and everything in the same mold."

One year later, writing in a prestigious American journal, another French Communist theoretician, Jean Kanapa, went one step further than Marchais. Eurocommunism was not merely a more democratic form of communism; it was a movement that would help expand and enrich French democracy and aid France in its present "crisis." France, he wrote, "must start on the right path toward democratic changes in her structures and in her objectives in every area. It is this uninterrupted extension of democracy which will lead the country to socialism, a socialism which must be authentically democratic."

What, then, is Eurocommunism, at least according to its own theorists and staunch supporters? It is a political philosophy shared by Communists in Spain, Italy, and France that stresses tolerance, social justice, and individual liberty. It supports peaceful, constitutional, and democratic change rather than violent revolution and dictatorship. And it rejects the notion—so long a part of the Communist movement in Europe and throughout the world—that the Soviet Union and the Russian Revolution of 1917 serve as the only models for Communist change and government. Where Soviet-style Communists have been known for their rigidity and strict adherence to party doctrine, Eurocommunists describe themselves as flexible, open, and willing to consider new ideas. Where Communists once claimed to possess the one true path to social justice and happiness, Eurocommunists now seem willing to listen to people with other ideas, and profess no monopoly of truth.

Political observers and the general public have been of two minds about Eurocommunism. On the one hand, many

The current leaders of the Western European Eurocommunist parties, from left to right, are: Georges Marchais of France, Santiago Carrillo of Spain, and Enrico Berlinguer of Italy.

men and women—for the most part political moderates and leftists of various parties—have welcomed its appearance. They believe that Eurocommunism represents a new "maturity" on the part of Western European communism, a maturity that has made genuine cooperation possible among parties once at odds with one another. Nino Pasti, for example, a retired four-star Italian general and former NATO commander, says he is convinced that the Communists are "fully reliable" and want to work within the democratic system.

On the other hand, more cautious or conservative individuals have contended that Eurocommunism must be viewed more critically and skeptically. The Eurocommunist commitment to tolerance and democracy, these critics warn, is too new and untested to be trusted. In the words of Jean Lecanuet, a moderate French politician, Eurocommunism may be nothing more than a mask worn by the Communists to make their parties more attractive and acceptable. If the Communists ever came to power, Lecanuet believes, this mask would be discarded and the true face of communism—dictatorial and violent—would be uncovered.

The United States and the Soviet Union have also been drawn into the controversy. Three American Presidents, Richard Nixon, Gerald Ford, and Jimmy Carter, have denounced Eurocommunism and warned that it poses a threat not only to American interests but also to the very survival of democracy in Western Europe. A victory for communism in Italy, France, or Spain, these Presidents believe, would undermine the ties that have bound these countries to America and would weaken the West's ability to defend itself against Soviet attack.

Nor has the Soviet Union found anything agreeable about the appearance of Eurocommunism. Eurocommunist leaders are regularly attacked in the Soviet press for their "crude anti-Sovietism" and for their "unsavory positions" and "slanderous allegations" against the USSR. Eurocommunism, writes one Soviet political theorist, is an invention of "bourgeois theorists" who know nothing about real communism. "There is only one communism—namely that whose foundations were laid by Marx, Engels, and Lenin and whose principles are adhered to by the present-day [Soviet] Communist movement." Eurocommunism, the Soviets believe, is a deviation and a heresy that must be brought under control before it becomes too strong.

Whatever attitude one takes toward Eurocommunism, however, there can be no doubt that the Eurocommunists have made promises and set goals for themselves that are drastically different from traditional communism. And, in a party where doctrine and words are so important and so constraining, says Annie Kriegel, a former Communist and leading French expert on communism, no change in language and doctrine can be considered a minor event. The Eurocommunists, she claims, have begun a basic transformation of party thought and practice that will play an important part in European political history.

This book will look closely at the origins of Eurocommunism and show how the Communist parties in Spain, Italy, and France have arrived at the positions they now hold. It will likewise survey both sides of the controversy over Eurocommunism—those who welcome its ideas and those who fear them—and detail the objections to the movement made by leading American and Soviet political theorists. The story that emerges is important and significant and will reveal much about European politics today, both conservative and radical, right and left.

In order to gain perspective, however, it will first be necessary to look into the Communist past. Eurocommunism is not completely new. Its commitment to human freedom and democracy, in fact, are deeply rooted in Communist history, a history that goes back well over one hundred years. We must look at the work of the founders of communism, Marx and Engels, and then at the changes and additions to their doctrines made by Lenin and Stalin. Only then can we see clearly which elements of that tradition the Eurocommunists have accepted, which they have rejected, and why they strive so hard to maintain their independence from Soviet-style communism and to prove their commitment to democracy.

CHAPTER TWO

MARX AND ENGELS

The founder and intellectual father of modern communism was Karl Marx. A prolific writer, astute social critic, and economist of note, Marx devoted his life to revolution and to the development of a system of thought which he believed would reveal the causes behind history, the reasons for human misery, and lead to the establishment of justice for all people. Few individuals have influenced subsequent generations more profoundly. Marx's ideas—which are often referred to collectively as Marxism—form the basis of political, social, and economic life in the Soviet Union, China, and Cuba. They are also a source of inspiration for many leaders in the developing nations of Africa and Asia and for the Eurocommunists of Italy, France, and Spain.

Marx's Early Life. Karl Marx was born in 1818 in the German city of Trier, the grandson of a rabbi and the son of a lawyer who had converted from Judaism to Protestantism.

Karl was educated in the schools of his native city and later at the universities of Bonn and Berlin.

From an early age, Marx displayed an unusual concern for justice and human suffering—a tendency he inherited from his father, who was a liberal and an advocate of constitutional reform in Germany. But he also showed a few of the more customary traits of a student of his time. He once fought a duel and on another occasion was arrested for drunk and disorderly conduct.

At the University of Berlin, Marx became acquainted with a circle of friends devoted to the philosophy of Georg Hegel. Hegel taught that all history was the progress of mind and reason from a primitive state of consciousness to a state of full consciousness where people would understand the nature of life and the meaning of such concepts as justice, beauty, and freedom. The mind could arrive at full consciousness, Hegel claimed, only after a long struggle that would cover many centuries; the end and goal of the struggle could only dimly be discerned at the beginning. One generation developed thought and reason to the fullest of its ability only to be confronted by a new generation with ideas and hopes of its own. Hegel called this process the dialectic; the thought of one age was rejected by the next but then given greater clarity and meaning by another, until humankind arrived, in time, at genuine truth and wisdom.

Hegel emphasized that his process was spiritual and that it took place in the mind. He was little interested in social change, politics, or economics. Marx, however, looked at things differently. He believed that Hegelianism offered a key to understanding human history but that Hegel had used that key wrongly. History for Marx was more than the growth of mind and consciousness; it was also the development of lib-

Karl Marx (1818–1883)

erty and democracy and social justice. The dialectic was the struggle of one generation after another to improve society to the point where genuine human freedom and happiness were possible. Hegel had seen freedom as primarily spiritual; Marx saw it as material—as the opportunity for all people to be free of want and free to exercise their talents and express their opinions.

Marx Moves to Paris. Spurred on by this new interpretation of Hegelian doctrine, Marx became editor of a liberal newspaper and published a series of editorials denouncing press censorship and promoting the causes of the poor. But soon the Prussian government, which Marx had severely attacked, suspended the newspaper and Marx decided to leave his native country. Already—it was 1843—he had grown dissatisfied with Hegelianism and believed that he needed contact with other systems of thought that offered different interpretations of reality.

Marx moved to Paris with his wife, Jennie, whom he had recently married. There he discovered a tradition of radical thinking practically unknown in Germany. France was the home of the French Revolution and of the heroes of that revolution: Saint-Just, Marat, Robespierre, Babeuf, and others long since dead but whose memories still played an active part in French attitudes. France was also the home of the Utopian Socialists Saint-Simon and Fourier, whose views enjoyed wide popularity among intellectuals, and of other Socialist writers who sought an end to the old order of society and the creation of justice and equality for all.

For Marx, these years in Paris were important. He read widely and edited a radical journal in German but also associated himself with groups of French and German working men who called themselves Communists but had no clear idea of what they meant by that term. Marx was moved by his new friends' sincerity and conviction and wrote, "The brotherhood of man is no mere phrase with them, but a fact of life." In Paris, too, Marx began his close association with a fellow German radical, Friedrich Engels, the son of a wealthy manufacturing family. It was an association that was to last the whole of Marx's life. Marx was the man of ideas who could look at history in the broad scope; Engels was the man of experience who could supply his friend with facts and useful information needed to make Marx's thoughts practical and down to earth.

The Communist Manifesto. In 1845, the French government—at the request of Prussia—asked Marx to leave Paris. He moved to Brussels, in Belgium, where he continued to write and to work with radical organizations. Two years later, while still in Brussels, he joined a secret London-based workers' organization called the League of the Just. The League soon changed its name to the Communist League and asked Marx and Engels to draw up a democratic constitution for it that would outline its goals. The result was the *Manifesto of the Communist Party,* the most dramatic and best-known document in Communist history.

Marx and Engels opened the *Manifesto* with a warning, "A specter is haunting Europe—the specter of communism." European society, it said, especially in the more advanced industrial countries, had reached the point where social and political change must take place. The *Manifesto* listed ten points where immediate action was necessary, ranging from the complete abolition of all inheritances and privately owned land to a graduated income tax and free education for all children. The Communists, it concluded, openly admit that their aims can only be achieved by a forcible overthrow of all existing conditions. "Let the ruling classes tremble at a Communistic revolution. The proletarians [workers] have nothing to lose but their chains. They have a world to win. Working men of all countries, unite!"

(15)

The *Manifesto of the Communist Party* was published in January 1848, a short time before revolutions broke out in France, Italy, Austria, and elsewhere. Marx went to Paris and then to Germany, where he played an active part in the events that were taking place. Fearful that extreme elements were taking control, Marx and Engels abandoned much that they had written in the *Manifesto* and insisted that the Communist League be disbanded. Instead, they wanted the working class revolutionaries to unite in common cause with liberal elements of other classes in order to establish a constitutional democracy. It was too soon for pure communism, Marx declared. Germany would first have to establish a middle-class democracy—one that would sponsor the expansion of industry and business—before a genuine Communist revolution could take place.

By the middle of 1849, however, Europe's revolutionary zeal had spent itself and the old order had returned to power. Marx left Germany for Paris, and then for London, where he remained the rest of his life except for short trips abroad. He now devoted himself to the completion of his system of thought and turned out numerous articles on a variety of social, economic, and political issues. Many of these articles were written for the *New York Tribune,* whose editor, Horace Greeley, had an interest in Socialist literature.

Das Kapital and Marx's Later Years. In 1867, Marx published the first volume of *Das Kapital,* the most important work in Communist history. Three later volumes were published after Marx's death. For many years while he was researching *Das Kapital,* Marx lived in the utmost misery and destitution. He and his wife and their four children shared a small two-room apartment and ate very little. Often their meals consisted of

Friedrich Engels (1820–1895)

only bread and potatoes. Engels helped them financially when he could, and after 1864, when he became a full partner in his family's firm, he was able to relieve their poverty with more liberal gifts of money and material goods.

Also in 1864, Marx ended his political isolation and once again began to take an active part in radical movements. He joined the International Workingmen's Association—more familiarly known as the First International—which had recently been formed in London and attended his first meeting on September 28. Soon after, he was asked to help draw up a constitution for the organization and to sit on its General Council. Over the next few years, Marx devoted a great deal of his time to the International, helping to settle disputes between various factions and giving advice where he could. By 1869, the International had more than 800,000 members throughout several European countries.

The last revolution to break out in Europe during Marx's lifetime was the Paris Commune of 1871. A few months earlier, Germany had invaded France and quickly defeated her. In the disruption that followed the short and humiliating war, the people of Paris took up arms, seized power in the city, and demanded that the government place controls on wages and prices and improve working conditions. Marx and Engels—who followed the events in Paris from their homes in England—believed that the Commune might be the first stage of a revolution that would destroy the capitalist societies of Western Europe and usher in the age of communism. They fully supported the insurrection, which nevertheless ended in a bloody defeat for the radicals two months after it had begun.

But the Paris Commune had nurtured and spread Marx's reputation as a revolutionary and it was a reputation that was to endure and grow as time passed. For the last twelve years of his life, Marx wrote little and suffered from poor health and from what he called "chronic mental depression." European Communists still asked him for advice from time to time, but he took no major part in radical politics after 1872, when he helped to resolve a dispute in the International Working Men's Association between a group of leftists, who wanted to bring revolution to Europe immediately, and his own followers, who believed it was necessary to wait until the time was ripe for revolution. The International itself lasted only four more years and was dissolved in 1876.

Marx died in 1883 and was buried in London. At his funeral, his friend Friedrich Engels said that Marx had accomplished two major things during his lifetime: He had discovered the laws that govern human history, and he had uncovered the workings of modern society. These were achievements, Engels said, that would last forever.

What Is Marxism? What were the laws of history that Marx claimed to have discovered? First, Marx believed that humans must be the focal point of all social thought. All human activity, he wrote, reveals that "For man, man is the supreme being." Man is a creature subject to needs that must be satisfied—hunger, shelter, clothing, and so on—and in the process of satisfying these needs, men and women over the centuries have created *by their own efforts* their technologies, their societies, their governments, their art, and their intellectual life. A person is a product of his or her own work and struggle, not the creation of a Supreme Being or some other agent.

Since a society is the creation of people, its benefits should be available to all who make up that society. But, Marx points out, this has not always been so. Centuries ago, there was a primitive communism where everything was shared and everyone was equal. But this benign state of affairs came to an end with the advent of private property. Thereafter, society became divided between the rich and the poor, the powerful and the weak. The rich and powerful came to own the means of satisfying people's needs—the land on which food was produced and the tools that made the manufacture of goods possible. They took control of the government and established laws and customs designed to maintain them in their dominant position. On the other hand, the poor and weak owned nothing and were powerless.

Marx theorized that history progressed in stages. Each stage was defined by two basic characteristics: (1) by the relationship between those who owned the means of production—by which he meant the means to satisfy human needs—and those who did not own the means of production, and (2) by the tools or machines available for people's use. The ancient world had its freemen, who were the owners, and its slaves; its tools and machines were simple and relatively unsophisticated. The medieval world was divided between lord and serf, while its characteristic tool was the handmill. In the modern world, the superior class was the capitalist class, and the inferior class was the workers. The machine that defined this stage of development was the steam mill, an invention that had revolutionized industry and had made the manufacture of goods on a large scale possible.

The class which controlled the means of production controlled society, dominated its politics and government, and determined the nature of its art and intellectual creations. History, society, and even the so-called higher forms of human study—philosophy, poetry, mathematics, and science—were, therefore, reflections of basic economic relationships. The ancient world reflected the relationship between freeman and slave, the medieval world the relationship between lord and serf, and the modern world the relationship between capitalist and worker.

But Marx also believed that history is a dynamic process. No one stage of history remains forever; each moves slowly and inevitably into the next, where new economic relationships are established, leading to new advances in society and thought. Eventually, a society develops its economy and social relationships to the point where further development is no longer possible in that stage. Then a new class of people, conscious of its rising strength and vitality, comes to power and replaces the older dominant class. This new class, in turn, reorders society and makes its own laws, politics, and morality.

His own time, Marx claimed, was witnessing the change from one stage of history to another. Capitalism reigned supreme in Great Britain, France, and, to a lesser extent, Germany. But capitalism had reached the point where it was ripe for change. It had advanced science, fostered the Industrial Revolution, established constitutional democracies, and improved the condition of humankind. But in spite of its successes, Marx concluded, capitalism was riddled with contradictions that would lead to its demise.

Capitalist society, for example, was rocked periodically with recessions and depressions that forced many men and women out of work. In addition, it protected the rich and tended to concentrate greater and greater wealth in fewer and fewer hands, while the ranks of the poor steadily increased. But perhaps the most demeaning characteristic of capitalism was its attitude toward the worker. Average workers earned low wages and worked long hours. Furthermore, they toiled to produce goods over which they had no control. The products of their own efforts were taken from them and sold to enrich the owners of the factories, the capitalists. In capitalist society, a person's strivings were owned by the capitalist class, which used them for its own benefit.

As Marx saw it, then, the dominant class of his time was the bourgeoisie—the industrialists, the bankers, the people who dealt in commerce and trade. The rising class was the workers, the group he called the proletariat. In the near future, Marx believed, the proletariat, after it had become well-organized and conscious of its own destiny as the next ruling class, would exert its power and seize control of the factories, the banks, and all the wealth now concentrated in the hands of a few. "The fall of the bourgeoisie," he wrote, "and the victory of the proletariat are equally inevitable."

Once the bourgeoisie had fallen, a "dictatorship of the proletariat" would follow, during which all vestiges of the old society would be destroyed. Private property would come to an end. Class antagonisms would disappear, because there would no longer be classes. The workers themselves would now own the factories and control the products of their own toil. "In the place of the old bourgeois society with its class struggles," Marx claimed, "there will be an association in which the free development of each man and woman is the condition of the free development of all."

In time, true communism would appear and the dictatorship of the proletariat would wither away, no longer needed. The whole person—unfettered by property or class distinctions and economically secure—would come into being. In the place of class ethics, there would be a human ethics, the same for each and every person. Humankind could return to the original happiness and emotional health it enjoyed in primitive society, but society would no longer be primitive. The wealth and resources of the world and the advantages of modern technology would be used for the benefit of all.

Marx and Revolution. Marx believed that the coming of communism was inevitable, just as the ancient world was destined to become the medieval world and the medieval world had to give way to capitalism. But at the same time he argued that intellectuals like himself could play a role in that change. It was the duty of the Communist party, he wrote, to help educate and organize the workers so that they would be prepared to take power when the time came. The foolish revolutionary, he said, thinks he or she can overthrow the old order at any time by taking up arms; the genuine revolutionary prepares, and waits for the right moment.

When he described how the final revolution would take place, Marx was of two minds. During his younger days, when he was filled with revolutionary zeal, he tended to think that violence was unavoidable. The old order, the dominant class, would not relinquish its power and wealth without a fight. The governments of Europe were too well entrenched and too strong to be overcome without the use of force. He once wrote, "We say to the workers, 'You have got to go through fifteen, twenty, fifty years of civil wars and national wars not merely in order to change your conditions but in order to change yourselves and become qualified for political power.' "

But there was another Marx, a Marx who had lived in Britain for many years and was impressed by parliamentary democracy. In his constitution for the International Working Men's Association, this Marx stressed the achievements of worker cooperation and the use of established legislative bodies to attain the goals and fill the needs of the proletariat. By gradually acquiring political power and working through the democratic system, Marx declared, the British workers might well achieve the society the Communists sought.

In 1895, twelve years after Marx's death, Friedrich Engels wrote in support of this side of Marxist doctrine. It was dangerous to believe, he said, that Communists could defeat the overwhelming military power of the modern state by resorting to arms. The Communists, he said, have their strongest and most invincible weapon in universal suffrage and the vote. What could never be achieved by violent class war could be achieved peacefully at the polls.

Marxism and the Eurocommunists. It is important to remember that neither Marx nor Engels believed that their writings were the last word that could be said on history and society. Marx looked upon his thought and philosophy as a tool to be used by the proletariat, a tool that would help the workers understand their role in history. Other writers and thinkers

(23)

would come along whose work would likewise aid the workers and help the cause of revolution.

"If there is one thing I am not," Marx said toward the end of his life, when he saw that his writings were being accepted as holy dogma by his followers, "I am not a Marxist." Marx and Engels believed that different societies would arrive at communism through different means. What was good for one nation might not be the best for another. Marxism could supply an outline for revolution and a means to understand social conditions, but it could not provide the definitive solution for all situations.

The Eurocommunists emphasize this more flexible, nondogmatic side of Marx's philosophy. They accept his critique of capitalist society and believe that communism is inevitable and desirable. But they also believe that the Marx who urged the proletariat to take up arms and prepare for war is not applicable to the Italy, Spain, and France of today. Instead, they look to the more democratic Marx, the Marx who was impressed by the achievements of the working class in democratic Britain. If Marx could believe that communism could be achieved by peaceful, parliamentary means in Great Britain, the Eurocommunists say, then the same means might work for democratic modern Europe.

CHAPTER THREE

THE TWO PATHS OF MARXISM: SOCIAL DEMOCRACY AND LENINISM

Since the time of Marx, Marxism has developed in two directions. The first path, that of the Social Democrats, took root in Germany during the last decades of the nineteenth century and has been the type of Marxism most popular in industrialized, democratic nations. The second path, Leninism, was responsible for the world's first Communist government—the Soviet Union—and has been the model for revolution most often followed by underdeveloped, oppressed nations. Both Marxist groups—the Social Democrats and the Leninists—claim to be the true heirs of Marx and Engels. But because the Leninists have been so successful, their claim has carried the greater weight.

The first Social Democratic party was founded in Germany in 1869. From the beginning it accepted Marx's doctrine of class struggle and his interpretation of history. At the same time, the party rejected violent revolution as outdated and unnecessary in a country where the workers could vote. The Social Democrats hoped to win power through the electoral process and by parliamentary means. In the meanwhile, they planned to gain gradual improvements for the working class by fighting for shorter working hours, better wages, and other benefits.

Under the leadership of August Bebel (1840–1913), the Social Democrats prospered. Bebel, who had been trained as a carpenter, ruled the party with an iron hand. The discipline he imposed on the membership helped to unify the party and make it possible for Social Democrats to play an important role in government in spite of efforts by the government to weaken them and defuse their strength. In 1877, the Social Democrats polled nearly 500,000 votes. In the elections of 1912, they won more than 4,000,000, making their party the largest single political party in Germany at that time. However, like the Eurocommunist parties of today, the Social Democrats found it difficult to achieve full power, in spite of their good showing, because of a coalition of moderate and conservative parties which opposed them.

The chief defender of orthodox Marxism among the Social Democrats was Karl Kautsky (1854–1938). As a young man, Kautsky had befriended Marx and throughout his life continued to regard the work and thought of the older man as the only true basis for social change and revolution. Like Marx, Kautsky believed that communism was inevitable. The rapid expansion of industrial society, the widespread improvements in technology, and the growth of the working class could only lead to the downfall of capitalism. The proletariat, well organized and conscious of its rights, would soon come to power and establish a new order.

Kautsky believed that democracy would play a central role in the coming of the Marxist revolution. "The conquest of political power by the proletariat," he wrote, "is of the highest value exactly because it makes possible a higher form of the revolutionary struggle." The battle for communism would no longer be a battle fought by unruly mobs that could be deceived and defeated.

"Democracy is indispensable as a means of ripening the proletariat for the social revolution," Kautsky continued. "Democracy is to the proletariat what light and air are to the organism; without them it cannot develop its powers." Yet democracy was not the final goal of Marxism, but rather a means to achieve that goal: "When the proletariat gains the first great victory over capitalism that places political power in its hands, it can use those powers in no other way than in the abolition of the capitalist system." Unless this is done, he warned, class antagonism will continue and society will forever be in a state of unrest. Once elected to office, the proletariat must proceed to use the governmental machinery to "bring about the most extensive social changes." Only then can the Marxist society be established.

In Eduard Bernstein (1850–1932), the German Social Democrats produced a second theoretician of note. Beginning from a purely Marxist position, Bernstein concluded that Marxism itself needed revision. Many of Marx's predictions, he argued, had not come true. The misery of the working class was not increasing; the number of wealthy people was not in decline. Nor were the periodic crises of capitalism—its depressions and recessions—growing worse and worse. Indeed, the condition of the poor and of the proletariat in Germany had improved, Bernstein pointed out, because the Social Democrats had worked through the political system to achieve their goals.

These conclusions led Bernstein to the notion that revolution itself was no longer needed. There was no need to destroy the democratic state in order to build socialism. By using the democratic state and preserving it, the workers could gain everything they needed and desired. Bernstein did not rule out the use of the general strike during times of severe crisis—a strike of all workers in every field of activity to bring the government to its knees—but he did believe that the proletariat could rely on peaceful and parliamentary means to influence government policy.

The Social Democrats played an important part in German political life in the last decades of the nineteenth century and the first years of the twentieth. Social Democrat parties imitating the German original spread throughout Europe— to Belgium (1885), Austria (1889), Poland (1892), Holland (1894), Russia (1898), and elsewhere. In 1889, the Second International Workingmen's Association—the first, in which Marx had participated, had come to an end in 1876— was established in Paris. By 1910, the Second International had grown to include delegates from twenty-three nations who met regularly to discuss social problems and plan political strategy. On the eve of World War I, social democracy was everywhere the dominant form of Marxism.

Marxism in Russia. The first major challenge to the dominance of the Social Democrats was to come from Russia. At the end of the nineteenth century, Russia was still a backward, underdeveloped nation, where industry had made few inroads. The vast majority of people were uneducated and superstitious peasants. The czar, the ruler of Russia, was an autocrat whose word was law. There were no democratic assemblies; there was no freedom of the press. The secret police, efficient and ever-watchful, kept an eye on all dissenters and attempted to destroy any movement that challenged the czar and his government. In short, Russia had none of the democratic institutions that helped to foster the growth of the Social Democrats in Germany and elsewhere in Western Europe.

Faced with this situation, revolutionaries in Russia formed secret societies dedicated to the use of violence and force. They assassinated many prominent military and government officials, including Czar Alexander II in 1881. But these societies, however dramatic and striking their actions may have been, were ineffectual. The young men and women who made up their numbers were too disorganized to be a major threat to the government and too impulsive to subordinate their need for immediate action and give higher priority to long-term planning and preparation.

In Nikolai Lenin, however, the Russian revolutionary movement found a leader of genius and a man who was willing to coordinate, plan, and wait for the right moment to strike. Lenin, who was born Vladimir Ulyanov in 1870 in the city of Simbirsk on the Volga, came from a family that was moderately well-to-do and educated. His father served as an important school official and was noted for the improvements he had made in the schools of his province.

The young Lenin was a very bright, capable student. He graduated at the top of his class. As a student, however, he showed no revolutionary interests, with the exception, perhaps, of his discovery at the age of sixteen that he had lost his faith in the Russian Orthodox church and was now an atheist.

Then, in 1887, Lenin experienced a tragedy that aroused his hatred of the czarist government and awakened his interest in radicalism. His beloved older brother, Alexander, was hanged along with several other conspirators for planning to assassinate Czar Alexander III. His brother's death came as a profound shock. Alexander, who had been a brilliant zoology student at the University of Saint Petersburg, was only nineteen. Lenin and his whole family fell under suspicion of the secret police. A family that fostered one revolutionary might well produce another.

By 1889, Lenin was avidly reading the works of Karl Marx and now considered himself a Marxist. Over the next few years, his commitment to revolution grew. Late in 1891, Lenin passed his university examinations, making excellent scores in every field. After the secret police lifted their objections, he was admitted to the bar and allowed to do legal work for the poor people of Samara, the city in eastern Russia where his family now lived. Firsthand experience with the lower classes and their problems gave Lenin further proof of the need for change and social improvement in Russia.

The year 1893 found Lenin in Saint Petersburg (today called Leningrad)—then the capital of the Russian Empire—where he joined a group of clandestine Marxists who called themselves the Union for the Struggle for the Liberation of the Working Class. The intention of the group was to spread Communist doctrine among the workers of the capital city. In 1895, Lenin and the other leaders of the group were arrested for their activities, imprisoned, and later sent into exile in a remote region of Siberia.

It was the first of several periods of imprisonment and exile that Lenin was to experience, none of which would dampen his revolutionary zeal. Banished from European Russia, he passed his time in study, in reflection on social problems, and in making plans for the future. As one of his political opponents was later to say, "There is no other man who is as absorbed by the revolution twenty-four hours a day, who has no other thoughts but the thought of revolution, and who even when he sleeps, dreams of nothing but revolution."

In 1900, Lenin, once again in exile, joined a group of Russians in Munich, Germany, who were members of the Russian Social Democratic party. Two years later, he published one of his most important revolutionary tracts. Entitled *What Is To Be Done?*, the essay elaborated an idea new to Marxist theory. In Russia, Lenin argued, revolution could only come by means of a small group, a party made up of highly disciplined, dedicated revolutionaries. This group would be centrally organized and composed of men and

Nikolai Lenin (1870–1924)

women willing to subordinate their own personal interests to the will of the party as a whole. The party members, he continued, would elect a central committee made up of individuals able to devote their entire time to revolution; they would have no career other than that of working for the party.

Further, Lenin wrote, this party would serve as "the vanguard of the proletariat." It would organize the workers, educate them in Marxist principles, and show them how to prepare for political power. But it would likewise *lead* and *guide* the proletariat in a way that Marx had not envisioned. For Marx, Communist doctrine and the Communist party were instruments to be used by the workers as they grew in political and social awareness. The revolution itself would be carried out by the masses of workers, organized and prepared to take control of the government. For Lenin, the small band of professional revolutionaries would be the agent of change and upheaval. Given the extreme backwardness of Russia, Lenin argued, a widespread and open revolutionary movement was unthinkable. Only a small group that acted as the *vanguard* of the proletariat, that worked in the forefront of the revolutionary movement and that was willing to take all matters concerning the revolution into its own hands could be successful.

In the years after the publication of *What Is To Be Done?*, Lenin set out to create the party he had in mind. He was often opposed by other Russian Social Democrats, who accused him of attempting to destroy open discussion within the party. His opponents—who at that time included Leon Trotsky, later to play an important part in the Russian Revolution—also feared that his position, if followed, would lead to a one-man dictatorship, a dictatorship *over* the proletariat, not a dictatorship *of* the proletariat. But in 1903, at a conference of the Russian Social Democrats in London, Lenin's ideas carried by a slim margin. The Bolsheviks, as followers of Lenin came to be known, after the Russian word for majority, came into favor while Lenin's opponents, the Mensheviks, or minority, took a back seat.

During the next nine years, attempts were made to heal the division between the Bolsheviks and Mensheviks, but to no avail. The Russian Revolution of 1905—a widespread rebellion of workers and peasants that began after Russia's defeat in the Russo-Japanese War—only widened the differences. During the revolution, the Mensheviks advocated cooperation with members of the Russian middle class. They believed that the country would have to experience a bourgeois revolution that would bring capitalism and democracy to Russia before a Communist revolution would be possible.

Lenin, on the other hand, took a distinctly different point of view. He argued that any alignment with members of the middle class was dangerous to the interests of the working class. Furthermore, he believed, the middle class was too weak in Russia to start a revolution. The Communists would have to depend on themselves and would have to overthrow the government on their own. At this same time Lenin added something new to the changes he had already made in Marxist doctrine. Given the special circumstances of Russia, he said, and its small numbers of workers, the revolution could not be the work of the proletariat alone, but must include large numbers of peasants. Marx had regarded the peasantry as unrevolutionary and unsympathetic to the interests of urban workers.

Leninism and World War I. The revolution of 1905 failed to destroy the Russian government, and the czar, by granting moderate reforms, remained in power. In 1912, the split between the Bolsheviks and Mensheviks became irreparable. Lenin maintained that he and the Bolsheviks represented the true party of revolutionary Marxism in Russia, but his influence had waned. The Mensheviks, with their more moderate policies, were now dominant.

Lenin never dreamed that the revolution he was working for would happen in his own lifetime. He looked upon himself as one who would help to pave the way for an upheaval that might not take place for perhaps another generation. What he had not foreseen was the outbreak of World War I.

The war, which began in August 1914, almost immediately discredited the Social Democrats of Germany and of the other European countries as being genuinely Marxist. In every parliament, a majority of Social Democratic delegates voted to support their nation's participation in the war. To most orthodox Marxists, this was heresy. It meant that the Social Democrats had placed national interests above class interests and were willing to see the workers of one nation fight and kill the workers of another nation. The influence of the Social Democrats went into rapid decline and pulled the Second International—which was supposed to have established fraternal ties and an international solidarity among workers—down along with it.

From Switzerland, where he now lived, Lenin opposed the war and kept a close watch on events in Russia, where things had gone badly almost from the beginning. In two and a half years, the Russian army suffered five and a half million casualties. The government at home found it difficult to feed and arm its soldiers, and throughout the country there was a shortage of food. The crisis came to a head in the early months of 1917 when Czar Nicholas II, an ineffectual leader, was dethroned and his government replaced by a democratic government, one that pledged to bring reform to the war-torn nation.

In April 1917 Lenin returned to Russia, determined to leave his imprint on the changes that were taking place there. He fully realized the difficult task ahead of him. The new government—called the Provisional Government—had the backing of many moderates and leftists, including the Petrograd * Soviet, an elected delegation of deputies from the factories of the capital city. And the majority of the members of the Petrograd Soviet were Mensheviks and others opposed to Lenin's ideas. Lenin, however, would accept no compromise with his opponents. From the moment he arrived in Russia, he demanded that the Provisional Government be overthrown and replaced with a more radical government and that Russia's participation in the world war be brought to an end.

Over the next few months, Lenin's views remained unpopular, and for a while he went into hiding, fearful of arrest. During this period, he wrote feverishly and authored an essay entitled *The State and Revolution,* which contained his views on what was happening in Russia. Up to 1917, he wrote, Marxists believed that a democratic system of government would work to bring about communism, just as it had helped to bring about capitalism. Democracy could be a tool of the proletariat, as it was now a tool of the bourgeoisie.

But the 1917 Revolution in Russia, Lenin maintained, had proved that this view was outmoded. The overthrow of the czar and the creation of the Provisional Government had been accomplished by the soviets—unions of workers, soldiers, and peasants. The major soviet existed in Petrograd, but others had sprung up throughout the country. These soviets—created spontaneously by the people—were truly representative of the proletariat and its needs. For the first time in history, the unpropertied classes had a strong and influential voice in public affairs. "All power to the soviets!" Lenin concluded. The soviets would lead armed peasants, soldiers, and workers who would "smash the machinery of government" and create a "dictatorship of the proletariat."

Near the end of October 1917, Lenin decided that the

* After the fall of the czar, the name of Saint Petersburg was changed to Petrograd. Later, after the Bolshevik Revolution, it was changed once again, this time to Leningrad.

time was ripe for action. Disappointment with the Provisional Government was now widespread. The war continued, food was still scarce, and few of the reforms promised after the fall of the czar had come about. The Bolsheviks had adopted a slogan of "Bread, Land, and Peace!" and were daily growing more popular. Lenin returned to Petrograd to take charge of his followers and to urge an immediate seizure of power.

On November 7 and 8, the final steps were taken. A militia formed by workers of the capital city, along with groups of revolutionary soldiers and sailors, forced the surrender of the Provisional Government. Power was turned over to the soviets and Lenin was elected head of the new government with the title of Chairman of the Council of People's Commissars. It might be noted here that at every step along the way to power, Lenin had been ably assisted by the former Menshevik, Leon Trotsky, who was now an ardent Leninist.

The job now was to stay in power and to finish the Revolution, and Lenin proved worthy of the task. With the support of the soviets, he confiscated the great landed estates of Russia and nationalized the banks. When the Mensheviks refused to cooperate with the new government on Lenin's terms, he dissolved the Constituent Assembly—a newly elected democratic legislature—in order to destroy their power. In March 1918 he concluded a peace that brought Russia's participation in World War I to an end.

Perhaps the greatest problem faced by the revolutionary government, however, was civil war. Large numbers of Russians—aristocrats, conservatives, and others—had never recognized Lenin's victory. Angered by the murder of the czar and his family and by what they feared would be the end of old Russia, these groups united to plan the overthrow of bolshevism. They were joined by contingents of troops from the Western nations—Great Britain, France, Canada, the

United States, and elsewhere. The West also supplied the anticommunist forces with weapons, ammunition, and money.

The Civil War that ensued cost millions of Russian lives and devastated the countryside, but Lenin remained firmly in power. He rallied the country behind him, milked resources for the war out of an economy that was in shambles, and created the Red Army under the leadership of Trotsky. He promised the peasants land and thereby gained their support. He promised the various nationalities that made up Russia—the Ukrainians, Georgians, Armenians, and others—the right to self-determination and thereby won their support, or at least their neutrality. It was Lenin's brilliant political leadership that saved the day for the Bolsheviks during the Civil War, as well as his willingness to make any move that would restore unity and preserve the Revolution.

Lenin in Power. Lenin remained at the head of the government for more than five years before he was incapacitated by a series of strokes that finally killed him on January 21, 1924. His regime was characterized by the same meticulous concern for detail and hard work that he had shown during his years in exile as the leader of the Bolshevik party. In foreign affairs, he sought to gain official recognition of the Soviet Union and its boundaries from a world that was often hostile to his revolutionary government. At the same time, however, he worked to strengthen the Communist movement abroad and bring it under Soviet control. At home, he took measures he believed would help to unify the country under the Communist party and bring about the eventual establishment of a genuinely Communist society.

In the first years after the Revolution, hopes were high among the Bolsheviks that the events in Russia would soon lead to revolution throughout the world. With this in mind, the Third International—an association of world Communist parties loyal to the Soviet Union—was formed in 1919. The International was to be the "main instrument for the liberation of the working class" and was to reflect Lenin's ideas of party organization. It was to be highly centralized and follow the notion of "democratic centralism," which meant that decisions would be reached through debate, but once reached, would be binding on every member.

Lenin listed twenty-one conditions that had to be met by each party that joined the International, or Comintern as it is often called. These conditions were meant to create a complete break with the traditions of social democracy and establish loyalty to the doctrines of Leninism. The new parties were supposed to adopt the name Communist party and declare their opposition to social democracy. They were to maintain a centralized and disciplined party press and to conduct regular purges of party ranks to remove members suspected of dissent and disagreement. They were also urged to carry on a systematic agenda of propaganda designed to win support from workers, peasants, and members of the armed forces. Any member party that failed to carry out these conditions would be thrown out of the Comintern and dismissed from the Communist movement.

At home, Lenin eventually turned to harsher methods to maintain unity and destroy opposition. Six weeks after the Revolution had taken place, he had overseen the establishment of a "commission for the suppression of counterrevolution." This commission rapidly developed into a secret police, which arrested dissenters and kept watch on suspected opponents of bolshevism. By 1922, Lenin was advocating frequent use of the death penalty. In a note to the Commissar of Justice, he wrote: "In my opinion, it is necessary to extend the application of execution by shooting to all phases covering the activities of Mensheviks and the like."

In 1921, Lenin announced his New Economic Policy, which was a step back from the "war communism" of the previous years, when the Soviet government maintained rigid control of the economy. The new policy encouraged private enterprise and gave the peasants the right to own their own land. It was not designed to be permanent, but a temporary state that would help stabilize society, encourage production, and increase the amount of available food.

The nature of the Bolshevik seizure of power and the bitterness of the Civil War helped to shape the character of communism in the Soviet Union. Lenin believed that the harsh measures he advocated and followed were necessary in order to overcome his enemies, who were many, and to secure the principles the revolutionaries had fought for. By his success, Lenin proved that revolution could come to a backward, poverty-stricken nation with little industry, a small working class, and no democratic tradition. And he had shown that the essential ingredient in the success of a revolution under these circumstances was a willingness to use force and to take measures that many people would find disagreeable. Force had deposed the Provisional Government and it had defeated the enemies of bolshevism during the Civil War. If the revolutionaries had shrunk from the use of arms and had relied on democracy and the vote, Lenin claimed, they would never have been victorious.

Lenin's triumph made his variety of communism the dominant interpretation of Marxism. Communist doctrine now came to be known as Marxism-Leninism, and the Russian Revolution became the chief model of Communist change and transformation. Revolutionaries throughout the world looked upon the Soviet Union as the homeland of Marxism and studied Lenin's tactics closely. Later, the excesses of Lenin's successor, Joseph Stalin, would call the achievements of the founder of bolshevism into question. Critics would accuse Lenin of planting the seeds of tyranny and oppression that made Stalin's regime possible. But for the time being, Lenin remained the supreme architect of communism.

CHAPTER FOUR

STALINISM AND ITS REBELLIOUS HEIRS

Karl Marx gave communism its doctrine and its method of looking at society and history. Lenin led the world's first successful Communist revolution. But it was Joseph Stalin who guided the Soviet Union to its leadership in international affairs and endowed communism with many of the qualities by which it is known today. For more than thirty years, Stalin's leadership of world communism was all-pervasive. Stalin became known as communism's pope and Moscow was his Rome. Stalin's combination of tyrannical rule, ruthlessness, and dedication to a single purpose turned Russia from a backward country into an industrial giant. But at the same time, it gave communism a heritage of dictatorship, violence, and terror that many Communists—including the Eurocommunists—would like to discard.

Stalin's Early Years. Joseph Dzhugashvili—he took the name Stalin from the Russian word for steel after he became a revolutionary—was born in 1879 in the Russian province of

Georgia. His family was very poor, but due to the insistence of his deeply religious mother, Stalin received a basic education at a church school and later attended a theological seminary where he studied to be a priest. The writings of Marx, however, began to attract his attention and before long he had become a full-time revolutionary. Stalin never developed the breadth of learning that had been characteristic of Marx and Lenin, nor did he ever travel widely in Europe as they had. His experience was almost entirely limited to the political and economic conditions of Russia and throughout his life, his point of view remained narrowly Russian.

Stalin's work in the revolutionary movement was varied. He attended several party conferences and was active in party affairs in his native province. But he made no name for himself until 1907, when he helped to organize a holdup in Tbilisi, the capital of Georgia. The holdup netted large sums of money for the Bolsheviks and gave Stalin a reputation as a man of action and commitment. In 1912, Lenin appointed him to a position on the party's Central Committee, but in July of the next year Stalin was arrested by the czarist secret police and sent to Siberia.

Stalin played an important role in the Bolshevik seizure of power in November 1917, and during the next few years he created a position of power for himself in the party and in the new Soviet state. He participated in the Civil War on several fronts as a military and political leader and at the same time held two high posts in the government: Commissar for Nationalities and Commissar for State Control. In 1922, he became Secretary General of the State Committee of the Communist party, and it was this position that eventually enabled him to become the absolute head of the Soviet Union and of the Communist party.

Joseph Stalin (1879–1953)

In 1922, however, Lenin was still alive and Stalin was only one of several possible successors to Lenin's power. Leon Trotsky, the man who had led the Red Army in the Civil War, a brilliant writer and an untiring revolutionary, was considered by many to be second only to Lenin in talent and ability. Others—including Grigori Zinoviev, Lev Kamenev, and the theoretician Nikolai Bukharin—were likewise highly regarded. Yet Stalin's power continued to grow, and by 1923, Lenin had grown deeply concerned about it. In a note which has come to be known as his "testament," Lenin warned the party leadership that Stalin had become too "rude" to hold the post of General Secretary and should be replaced by a man who was "more patient, more loyal, more polite, and more attentive to comrades, and less capricious." Two months later, he dictated a second note to his secretary which announced his severance of "all personal and comradely ties" with Stalin.

But by this time, Lenin was a sick man. Two strokes had racked his body late in 1922 and diminished his abilities. More strokes followed in 1923, which forced him into retirement, isolated him from his comrades, and rendered him unable to control the events that were taking place. When Lenin died in January 1924, Stalin still held a position of power in the government.

Stalin in Power. In 1927, Stalin emerged victorious over all his rivals. Trotsky was the first to fall in disgrace, followed by Zinoviev and Kamenev, and then by Bukharin. At first satisfied with rendering these men powerless, Stalin later eliminated them entirely. Zinoviev and Kamenev were forced to give up their party memberships and were then reinstated among the rank and file after a humiliating admission of their "mistakes"

Leon Trotsky (1879–1940)

and "errors." In 1936, they were executed, along with Bukharin. Trotsky experienced a somewhat different fate. Banished from the Soviet Union in 1929, he was assassinated in Mexico City in 1940 by a Stalinist agent.

With the elimination of Stalin's rivals, the true nature of Stalinism began to emerge. Since the death of Lenin, Stalin had urged what he called "socialism in one country." It had become obvious, he argued, that communism had failed to take root in other countries and that the world revolution the Bolsheviks had hoped to initiate would not come about for some time. It was therefore the duty of the Soviet Union to build a strong, invincible homeland for communism that would serve as an example for the whole world. Once genuine military and industrial power had been achieved, then the USSR could compete with the capitalist nations on an equal basis and eventually overtake them, thereby proving the superiority of communism. "We are fifty or a hundred years behind the advanced countries," Stalin said. "We must make up this gap in ten years. Either we do it or they crush us."

In 1928, Stalin announced the "First Five-Year Plan," a rigorous agenda of economic and social change designed to be the initial step in the modernization of Soviet life. The plan called for the complete regimentation of Soviet society. Work, discipline, and self-sacrifice would be expected of every citizen; order and unity would characterize the nation as a whole. All authority would come from above, from Stalin, whose word was law. For the sake of unity and singleness of purpose, dissent would not be tolerated. Every resource of the state—the military, the secret police, and the use of terror—would be harnessed to enforce the wishes and policies of the dictator and to keep all individuals on the course he had set.

In several ways, Stalin's First Five-Year Plan and similar plans which followed it were highly successful. Heavy industry, steel plants, and new factories sprang up out of nowhere. New power plants supplied the energy necessary for economic expansion. The production of coal, iron ore, and other resources rose rapidly. The optimistic slogan of the period was "There are no fortresses which Bolsheviks cannot take," meaning that there was no problem they could not solve. Party officials boasted that the vitality of the Soviet economy would surpass even that of the American economy by 1937.

However, the price paid by the Soviet people in hardship and suffering for Stalin's industrialization efforts was huge. The peasants suffered most. Millions—some estimates are as high as twenty-five million households—were forced from their homes and land and moved to state-owned collective farms. Those who resisted were shot, exiled, or sent to concentration camps. Many other peasants moved to the cities to find work in the new factories only to find that wages were low and the housing inadequate. The widespread disruption of life in the countryside resulted in a marked decline in agriculture. The food supply grew scarce and sections of the country experienced famine. Yet Stalin refused to modify his plan.

Life for the people of the cities was also difficult. Stalin's emphasis on the development of heavy industry resulted in an uneven and unstable economy. Machines were produced, while consumer goods were nowhere to be found. The standard of living fell and the average worker was worse off in 1933 than he or she had been in 1929. By 1934, social unrest and dissatisfaction had caused many Russians to doubt the wisdom of Stalin's rule. A movement among Communist party members gained momentum and sought to limit the power of the dictator by forcing him to share his position as General Secretary with other prominent Communists.

The Purges and World War II. Stalin, however, would accept no challenge to his authority. Working carefully but decisively, he began to plan the elimination of the opposition. His chance came in 1934 when his chief rival, Sergey Kirov, was assassinated in Leningrad. No one knows for certain if Stalin had Kirov killed, but in the months that followed the murder, Stalin used it as a pretext for a thorough "cleansing" of the party. No one was above suspicion. Stalin and his personal associate, N. I. Yezhov, the Commissar for Internal Affairs, pretended to find enemies of the Soviet nation in all ranks of society, among old revolutionaries who had participated in the Bolshevik seizure of power, high army officers, and at all levels of the party hierarchy.

The Great Purge, as this period in Russian history is called, reached its peak in 1936 and 1937. Numerous men and women—the exact number will probably never be known—were arrested for making anti-Stalinist remarks or for having associated with groups loyal to Stalin's rivals. Many were given highly publicized trials where they confessed their "guilt" and were sentenced to prison or to death. Many others were simply executed or sent to concentration camps and never heard from again. Nearly half the total party membership was eliminated during the purge, as were 57 of 85 corps commanders of the Red Army and 110 out of 195 of its divisional commanders.

When the new Party Congress—the 18th—assembled in Moscow in 1939, each delegate realized that more than half the number of delegates to the previous Congress were now dead, victims of Stalin's wrath. Stalin had achieved his aim. He now remained in absolute control of the party and the government; no one dared to question his authority. The Party Congresses, which had been held at regular intervals, were abandoned and a new Congress did not meet until 1952. Stalin ruled through trusted agents and the secret police.

In the years after Lenin's death, Stalin also brought the world Communist movement under his strict control and regimentation. Policies for the Communist parties of every nation were determined in Moscow and the local parties were expected to carry out these policies without question. When the headquarters of the Communist International in the Soviet Union announced a change in party strategy, other parties likewise had to alter their activities and tactics. In addition, each party was required to organize itself as Stalin had organized the USSR, with power concentrated at the top and no dissent permitted among the rank and file.

Between 1924 and the outbreak of World War II, four different lines of action—often totally opposed to one another —were pursued by world communism:

(1) 1924–1928: The period of the United Front. All Communist parties were ordered to cooperate with other parties of the left in order to weaken right-wing movements. At the same time, every party was expected to eliminate from its ranks anyone who opposed Stalin.

(2) 1928–1935: The period of isolation. The parties were told that it was the duty of Communists everywhere to support the Soviet Union by every available means. Communist parties were to remain aloof from all other parties and pursue only a purely Communist line. This policy was disastrous in Germany, where the large German Communist party, following Soviet orders, refused to join other parties of the left to prevent Hitler's rise to power.

(3) 1935–1939: The period of the Popular Front. The Communist parties of the world were now ordered to work with Socialists and other parties of the left and middle in order to destroy fascism and nazism, which had come to power in Italy and Germany. The Popular Front strategy was effective for a while in France, where the Communists united with the Socialists and moderates in 1936, and in Spain, where the Communists cooperated with other parties to preserve the Spanish Republic.

(4) 1939–1941: The Hitler-Stalin Pact. In an abrupt turn-about, Stalin signed a treaty with the German dictator that allowed the two leaders to divide Poland between them and gave Lithuania, Estonia, and Latvia to the Soviet Union. In return, Hitler promised not to invade Russia. All Communist parties were required to recognize fascism and nazism as "lesser evils" than capitalism and to cease their cooperation with other parties of the left.

Stalin's regimentation of world communism had two general effects. On the one hand, it made each individual Communist party appear to be a mere tool or agent of Soviet propaganda and policy. By pursuing the Moscow line so closely, the various national Communist parties seemed to show greater concern for the interests of a foreign nation than for the needs and policies of their own countries. Their national loyalty could be—and often was—called into question by anticommunists, while other parties of the left could—and often did—deplore the "spinelessness" of a party that seemed to have no ideas of its own.

On the other hand, Stalin's control helped to unify the Communist movement and to give it a singleness of purpose it may not have acquired if each national party had been allowed to establish its own plans and strategies. At no time was this unity and singleness of purpose more beneficial than during World War II. When Hitler invaded the Soviet Union in June 1941, Stalin immediately abandoned his pact with Germany and called on Communists everywhere to join the nations of the West and work for the destruction of Nazi Germany, Fascist Italy, and their ally Japan.

During World War II, the prestige of world communism reached its highest point. The people of the USSR suffered greatly during the war, but they managed to survive and carry on the struggle in spite of the German occupation of much of their country. In France, Italy, and Yugoslavia, Communists actively participated in underground movements and guerrilla bands. In 1943, when Stalin announced that he had dissolved the Communist International, it appeared that he had abandoned his earlier denunciation of the capitalist nations for an era of cooperation and toleration. Stalin himself declared that it was not his wish to bolshevize other nations. His only aim, he said, was to preserve the security and dignity of his own country.

The Postwar Years. But the era of cooperation and mutual tolerance was short-lived. At the end of the war (1945), Stalin emerged stronger than ever, feared by many of his people but also revered as the man who had led the Soviet Union to victory. At home, he began to initiate plans to restore the damage done by the war; abroad, he turned with interest toward Europe, where widespread destruction and social upheaval seemed to make an expansion of Soviet influence more viable. This was especially true in the case of the nations of Eastern Europe—Poland, Hungary, Czechoslovakia, Romania, and Bulgaria—that had been liberated from German occupation by the Red Army and which were geographically near the Soviet border.

The first postwar governments in these countries had been formed by coalitions of Socialists, liberals, Communists, and other political parties pledged to rebuild their war-torn nations. Everywhere the Communists promised to abide by parliamentary rules and to guarantee individual liberty. In Hungary, the Communist leader, Erno Gero, declared that "The Communist party does not approve of the idea of a one-party system. Let the other parties operate and organize as well." And in East Germany, a party official promised "a parliamentary democratic republic with full democratic liberties."

One by one, however, the Communist parties of Eastern Europe took complete control of the governmental apparatus in their countries and ousted the other parties. Leaders sympathetic to Stalin were placed in power and a Stalinist-type dictatorship was established. Noncommunists were exiled, imprisoned, or murdered, while each country as a whole was forced into the rigid pattern of economic and social development followed in the Soviet Union. The two exceptions were Yugoslavia and Albania, where communism had been established by native Communist movements, often as harsh in their methods as Stalinism but outside the control of the Soviet leader.

The creation of Communist regimes in Eastern Europe added nearly 100 million people to the ranks of those living under communism. With the victory of the Chinese Communists—who had been supported by Stalin—and the establishment of Mao Tse-tung's government in 1949, fully one-third of the world's population was Communist-ruled. Stalinism was at the peak of its success and its achievements had been striking. In two decades, it had turned Russia from a backward country into a major world power. Industrialization and modernization had changed the face of Soviet society forever. Germany had been defeated and the principles of Marxism-Leninism, as interpreted by Stalin, had been extended to other nations. Indeed, Stalin could claim, with some justification, that he had surpassed both Marx and Lenin as the greatest revolutionary and strongest leader of the party.

Stalinism is Challenged. In 1949, few people could have known that Stalin's influence and prestige would decline rapidly over the next few years. Even at the time of his death—on March 5, 1953—he still seemed strong and invincible. However, two major challenges to his authority had already appeared, and, in time, these challenges would undermine the momentum of Soviet expansion and destroy the unity of world communism.

One of these challenges came from the West. In the years

after World War II, the democratic nations, led by the United States, grew deeply concerned about the spread of the Communist "menace." This concern quickly grew into a fear that Stalin would eventually control the whole of Europe and much of the rest of the world unless he was stopped. The noncommunist nations began to arm themselves and to prepare for a confrontation. American aid helped to rebuild a war-ravaged Europe, while American diplomacy and military power were used to establish a worldwide barrier to Communist advance.

The result was what was known as the Cold War, a rapid buildup of arms and weapons—including large stockpiles of nuclear bombs—and an increase of tensions between East and West. Yet Stalin's power was checked. In 1948, when he attempted to seize the city of Berlin—which had been divided into Western and Soviet sectors at the end of World War II—the determination of the democratic nations to preserve the freedom of the Western sectors was successful. Stalin backed off, in order to avoid war.

The second challenge to Stalin's power and influence came from the Communist world itself. In 1948, the same year as the Berlin Crisis, the Communist leader of Yugoslavia, Marshal Tito, had a quarrel with Stalin over the role the Soviet Union was to play in Yugoslavia. The immediate cause of the quarrel was the establishment in 1947 of the Communist Information Bureau (Cominform) with its headquarters in Belgrade, the Yugoslav capital. The Cominform was a union of the Communist parties of the USSR, France, Italy, and the Eastern European nations. It had been formed to bind these parties more closely together and to coordinate their activities.

Tito feared that the Cominform would mean Soviet domination of Yugoslavia. Moreover, he considered the Yugoslav Communist party to be an independent party that had waged a successful guerrilla war against the German occupation of

Yugoslavia and thus owed little to Stalin or the Soviet Union. He refused to submit to the Cominform and turned a deaf ear to Stalin's demands for cooperation. For a while, it seemed that Stalin might order the Red Army to invade Yugoslavia to force Tito's surrender. But the invasion never came. Tito survived the crisis and was the first Communist leader to stand up to Stalin and maintain his independence.

Tito's victory was a momentous event in the history of the Communist movement. It meant that the monolithic control of the Soviet Union over world communism had been broken. It meant that a type of communism different from the kind followed in the USSR would be allowed to take root and develop according to its own plans and needs. In the years that would ensue, Yugoslav communism would take a course similar to that envisioned by Lenin. There would be more participation by workers and peasants in the control of factories and farms and less emphasis on centralized control of every aspect of economic and social development. The Yugoslav state would be restrictive and dictatorial, but Tito's power would never reach the proportions achieved by Stalin.

Khrushchev and De-Stalinization. Eventually Stalinism was discredited by the Soviets themselves. In 1956, the new General Secretary of the Communist party, Nikita Khrushchev, used the occasion of the 20th Party Congress to denounce his predecessor in terms usually reserved for capitalists or other enemies of communism. Stalin, Khrushchev declared, had been a tyrant whose excesses had harmed the Communist cause. He had ruled by personal whim and had created around him a "cult of personality," a cult that made Stalin's own name synonymous with communism and ignored the needs and desires of the Communist party as a whole.

Josip Broz Tito (1892–   )

In his speech—which was made before an assembly of Communist delegates from all over the world—Khrushchev likewise announced a new Soviet attitude toward Communist revolution and social change. Stalinism had tended to emphasize the necessity for violence and force in establishing a Communist government and had supported Mao Tse-tung's war in China as well as urged the French and Italian Communist parties to strike and create disorder in their respective countries. Khrushchev now declared that parliamentary democracy could serve as a "form of transition to communism" and that violence or terror were not always necessary. Two months later, on a visit to Yugoslavia where he attempted but failed to patch up Soviet disagreements with Tito, Khrushchev further confirmed this doctrine. "The conditions of Communist development are different in different countries," he said. No Communist country had the right to impose its views on another.

Khrushchev's denunciation of Stalin opened a new era in the history of the Communist movement. National Communist parties were given an independence that they had not previously had. The days were gone when the Communist International could require its members to support the Soviet Union in every way possible. The Communist parties of the world now seemed bound by a common commitment to the ideas of Marx and Lenin, rather than by their submission to a Soviet dictator.

In the years that followed Khrushchev's speech, the Soviet Union did not always live up to the promises Khrushchev made. Indeed, Khrushchev himself was the first to violate his pledges. He took steps to maintain rigid Soviet control of Poland in 1956, at a time when the Poles were restless and asking for economic and political changes. A few months later, he sent the Soviet army into Hungary to put down a rebellion there against Soviet domination. And once again, in 1968, a new leader of the Soviet Union, Leonid Brezhnev, used the army to destroy the liberal Communist government of Czechoslovakia when it threatened to pursue policies vastly different from those of the USSR.

But on the whole, Soviet policy did not return to the days of Stalinism. At home, Soviet society continued to be oppressive and totalitarian, but the days of Stalin's purges, the mass arrests, show trials, and mass executions were gone. Nor was the Soviet Union able to maintain its control of world communism. Tito continued his independent course in Yugoslavia, while a quarrel between the Soviet Union and Communist China in 1959 developed into a second split in the Communist movement, a split that has never healed.

Today, the idea of a monolithic Communist empire—everywhere and at all times the same—is a thing of the past. China and Yugoslavia have gone their own ways. Romania has launched an independent foreign policy unthinkable in the time of Stalin. Even Poland and Hungary, still under Moscow's watchful eye, have been allowed to pursue social and economic goals that vary somewhat from traditional communism.

The Eurocommunist movement represents yet another split in world communism.

The ideas that were to form the basis of Eurocommunism first appeared in Western Europe long ago. They took root in the years of de-Stalinization following Khrushchev's speech before the 20th Party Congress and began slowly to mature. In each party, the emphasis was the same—to root out the policies and habits of thought that had been established during the Stalinist years and return to a Marxism that was less rigid and more adaptable to changing circumstances. It is now time to look separately at the Communist parties of Italy, France, and Spain and to see how they arrived at Eurocommunism.

CHAPTER FIVE

EUROCOMMUNISM IN ITALY

The Italian Communist party (PCI) is the largest Communist party in the noncommunist world. With almost two million members, it permeates almost every aspect of Italian life. There are powerful Italian Communist trade unions and influential Italian Communist youth groups. For many years, several large Italian cities, such as Bologna, have had Communist mayors and Communist city governments that have earned a reputation for efficiency and good administration. Italian Communist organizations publish books, newspapers, and magazines and are active in other forms of the communication media. Experts agree that the PCI may well be the first Eurocommunist party to come to national power and to have its members chosen for Cabinet-level posts.

The Origins of Italian Communism. The PCI was first established in 1921 during a time of trouble, when Italy was on the verge of civil war. In the following year, the Fascist dictator, Benito Mussolini, seized control of the country and before long outlawed all parties but his own. Communist leaders and party members were harassed and arrested. Many were killed or forced into exile. For the next two decades, the party remained underground, a secret and illegal organization with a small number of dedicated members.

One of the Communists imprisoned under Mussolini was Antonio Gramsci, the intellectual father of the PCI. Gramsci was arrested in 1926 and not released until 1937, shortly before his death. During his years of freedom and through his writings while in prison, Gramsci elaborated a doctrine that has become widely influential. Italy, he said, was a Catholic nation and communism would have to recognize this fact. But, he added, the Communists could use the immense power of Catholicism in Italy by working *within* the established political and social system and in time replacing the authority and leadership of the Church with the authority and leadership of Marxism.

How would this come about? By pulling the Church into the political arena, Gramsci answered. Once the Catholic Church entered the world of practical politics, the Communists could meet it on their own terms and defeat it. In Gramsci's words, "Catholicism would emerge from a narrow hierarchy and become part of the crowd." By so doing, the Church would "commit suicide." It would become part of the corrupt social and governmental system and lose its spiritual hold over the masses of Italian people, who would then look for something to replace it. Marxism would be that replacement. Like Catholicism, Marxism offered a *total* view of the world, a view that could fill all the old religious needs that had become outmoded and behind the times.

Instead of a Leninist-style immediate seizure of power by the Communists, Gramsci advocated a gradual movement that would eventually absorb all the political, social, and economic institutions of the nation. In the first phase of this revolution, the Marxists would work with reformers and radicals of all parties in order to create a secular and antireligious tradition among the nation's intellectuals. In the second phase, the Marxists would use the Catholics to help dismantle the structure of the "bourgeois state" and pave the way for communism. In short, Communists would first turn their attention to winning the society and its culture; then they would overtake the state. This was Leninism in reverse. Lenin had seized the state apparatus in order to transform society; Gramsci would leave the state until last, after the hearts and minds of the Italian people had already turned to communism.

World War II and The Postwar Years. It was during World War II that the PCI first began to play a significant role in Italian society. The Communists, who supported the Committee for National Liberation, a group made up of liberals, Socialists, and others dedicated to the overthrow of fascism, fought against the Nazi German and Italian Fascist troops that controlled the country and supported the American troops after the Allied invasion of Italy.

As a result, an era of good will followed the end of the war. Liberals, Socialists, Communists, and others joined together in an effort to create a democratic government and erase the Fascist past. Communists held important government posts and found growing support for their party at the polls. In the elections of June 1946, nearly one-fifth of the Italian electorate voted Communist.

The era of good feeling came to an end in 1947. The expansion of Soviet influence in Eastern Europe threw suspicion on Communist aims everywhere. The PCI found itself regarded with mistrust and fear by conservatives and moderates who thought that Stalin might send the Red Army into Italy. The Communist leaders who had played a role in the early postwar government now found themselves excluded from power by their former friends and collaborators. The United States offered money and aid to rebuild the country with the understanding that the Communists would share no part of the new Italy. Under the leadership of Alcide de Gasperi, the Christian Democrats—a party comprised of conservatives, moderates, and liberals united by their Catholic faith—assumed complete control of the government and vowed to keep Italy on a democratic course. Only the Italian Socialist party (PSI) maintained its former relationship with the Communist party.

Excluded from power, but not outlawed, the PCI endured the crisis of the Cold War and proceeded to regain its influence. Under the leadership of Palmiro Togliatti, the party had already begun to pursue a course that varied from the policies of other Communist parties. Italian communism, Togliatti argued, could be successful only if it became a mass movement and joined the mainstream of Italian life. In this notion, he was at one with Gramsci, the party theoretician. The PCI should have members from all walks of life and from all social and economic classes. It should reflect the needs and interests of society as a whole.

Under Togliatti's leadership, party membership rose from an estimated 6,000 in 1943 to more than 2.3 million in 1951—a rate of almost 300,000 new members a year. This phenomenal growth altered the character of communism in Italy. Instead of a comparatively small, secret organization—based on Lenin's ideas of party structure—the PCI developed into a large and highly visible party. The large number of Italian Communists made possible the representation of a variety of opinions within the party and rendered complete control of the membership—in the manner of Stalin—a difficult task.

Palmiro Togliatti, one of the first Italian Communist leaders to break from traditional communism.

(62)

Togliatti and De-Stalinization. In 1948, Togliatti refused to join Stalin and other Communist leaders in condemning Tito's independent course of action in Yugoslavia. Tito, he declared, should have the right to establish the sort of Communist society he believed best for his own country. But it was not until 1956 that the full extent of Togliatti's differences with Stalin became known. In that year, the Italian Communist leader defended Nikita Khrushchev's attack on Stalin's errors and excesses. Like Khrushchev, Togliatti believed that Stalin had ruled by a "cult of personality" and had disregarded the wishes of the party rank and file in order to set himself up as a dictator.

But Togliatti went further than Khrushchev in his condemnation of Stalin. Stalin's rule, he said, had caused the "stagnation of the masses" by weakening the trade unions and the factory soviets. Stalin had governed beyond the bounds of legality and his purges of party ranks had been "censurable on a moral basis." Furthermore, Stalin had supervised the growth and expansion of a vast bureaucracy that stultified social and economic change in the Soviet Union. In his last years, Lenin had warned the party against such a bureaucracy, saying that it would undermine the achievements of the Revolution. Stalin had chosen to ignore this warning and the result was a massive governmental apparatus that slowed down the development of a genuine Communist society.

The only ways to develop genuine communism, Togliatti claimed, was to establish "a proper democratic life both in the party and in the state" and to maintain "permanent and close contact with the popular masses in all walks of life." Italian communism, he promised, intended to do just that. By moving on democratic grounds and "without leaving those grounds," he said, the PCI could help perfect Italian democracy. "It will be for us to work out our own method and life in order that we, too, may be protected against the evils of stagnation and bureaucratization [that afflicted the Soviet Union under Stalin]."

Togliatti called his doctrine "polycentrism," which meant that the Communist movement would have many centers of development, as many as there were Communist parties throughout the world. Italian Communists would follow their own path to communism and would expect other Communist parties to do the same. The PCI would work within the parliamentary system and would defend the right of every individual to worship as he or she saw fit. Italian communism saw no need to resort to violent revolution, but would come to power peacefully and gradually. Togliatti had maintained many of these positions since World War II, but his restatement of them during the period of de-Stalinization helped to give them new force and significance. Under his influence, Italian communism chose a path very different from the communism of the Soviet Union, a path that would eventually lead to Eurocommunism.

The Opening to the Left. The staunchly anticommunist government established by Alcide de Gasperi in 1947 lasted only six years. By 1953, the Christian Democrats had lost their majority in parliament and needed to find support from other political parties in order to form a new government. De Gasperi had characterized the Christian Democrats as a party of the middle which was moving to the left, but he first turned to Italy's small right wing Monarchist party for help. The ensuing protest from the left wing of his own party caused him to abandon negotiations with the Monarchists and to initiate a turn to the left.

At first, the move to the left went slowly. The Christian Democrats sponsored progressive legislation that increased government spending in many areas popular with leftists: public schools and hospitals, transportation, and so on. These moves increased the party's appeal to voters, but still the electoral majority remained elusive and the Communists were making increasingly good showings. Between 1958 and 1960, many Christian Democrats came to the conclusion that it was necessary to establish what they called an "opening to the left." By this they meant that the Christian Democrats should seek a coalition with the PSI—Italy's small but influential Socialist party—in order to create a stable government.

The argument in support of the coalition took the following form. The Socialists were a Marxist party, but were nevertheless strongly on the side of individual liberty and freedom. The Christian Democrats could associate with them without fear that democracy would suffer. At the same time, Christian Democrat and PSI collaboration would weaken the Italian Communist party by pulling the Socialists away from the Communists, thereby leaving the Communists isolated on the far left. Furthermore, the combined Socialists and Christian Democrats would pass a broad slate of Socialist measures that would undermine support for the Communists and erode their power base.

That was the opening to the left as seen from the eyes of the Christian Democrats. The Communists, however, viewed it differently. As early as 1955, Togliatti looked upon the Christian Democrat move to the left as an opportunity for his party. He hoped that the Christian Democrats would be forced to accept the Socialists as partners and that eventually the opening to the left would become so wide that the Christian Democrats would be forced to deal with the Communist party. Instead of accepting this as a push into isolation and stagnation, Togliatti saw it as an opportunity to expand Communist influence.

Events bore out Togliatti's view of the situation. When the opening to the left took hold in the early 1960s, it did not bring political stability for the Christian Democrats and a decline in the Communist vote. On the contrary, the opposite happened. The Communist party began to enjoy a rapid increase in popularity, while the Christian Democrats gained nothing and were forced to continue their search for political allies in order to prop up their minority government.

The search for an ally moved the Christian Democrats further and further to the left until Togliatti's prediction came true. The Christian Democrats began negotiations with the Communists. The sequence of Christian Democrat slogans from 1947 to 1968 reflects this change in attitude. During the Cold War the de Gasperi government had spoken of an "Anticommunist Crusade." Later Christian Democrat slogans emphasized the "Irreducible Contest" and the "Very Clear Distinction" between the Christian Democrats and the Communists. But by the late 1960s, the Christian Democrats were talking about "Democratic Competition" and "Constructive Dialogue" between the two parties. The PCI had moved from its position as an outcast to the forefront of Italian politics in a period of twenty years.

The Reasons Behind the Communist Success. One of the reasons the PCI was able to turn the opening to the left to its advantage was that the opening itself enjoyed widespread support in the news media and among liberals and moderates. The opening was seen not so much as a way to *stop* the PCI as it was regarded as a means to bring the Communists into the democratic system. In 1962, a leading Italian newspaper declared, "Those democrats most committed to and most concerned with the future naturally turn their attention to integrating the masses and the leadership of the PCI into the life of the state."

A large segment of important political opinion was therefore behind the opening to the left and wanted to see it work. In the minds of many people, Italy's Fascist past was still a grim reality, and a strong move away from the right was seen as proof that the country would never again lapse into fascism.

The PCI, as any political party would, took advantage of this situation to increase its own prestige. If the public accepted a move to the left that would include the Socialists and later the Communists, the PCI would not be the party that said no.

A second reason for the expansion of Communist power was the attitude of the Socialist party. When the Christian Democrats began to pursue the opening to the left, they received assurances from the Socialists that the Socialist party would take steps to sever its connections with the Communists. But this was not to be. In spite of their collaboration with the Christian Democrats, the Socialists continued to maintain their ties with the Communists in the trade unions, in local party organizations, and elsewhere.

Indeed, when the PSI joined the Christian Democrats in a new government in 1963, it called for a "broadening of the base of the majority," by which it meant that the Communists should be included in the Cabinet. In the years that followed, the Socialists continued to maintain this position. As a result, the Communists were never isolated from political life, as the creators of the opening to the left had hoped they would be. Instead, the PCI was drawn more and more into the political arena and was regarded with less and less distrust and fear.

But behind the PCI's success was a third factor that should be taken into consideration. The party was well-organized and politically experienced. Over the years, it had gained widespread influence in the Italian trade union movement and in many other aspects of Italian life. It could count on the support of large numbers of voters and it included within its ranks a sizable number of professional party members—men and women who had made party work their career and who understood the workings of the Italian political system and Italian society. Without this corps of dedicated, disciplined members, the PCI could never have achieved the authority and influence that it did.

The Social and Economic Instability of Italian Society. In the 1960s and 1970s, three grave social and economic problems helped the Communists in their drive for power. The first was unemployment, coupled with a high inflation rate. In the 1950s and early 1960s, the Christian Democrats had presided over one of the greatest economic booms in Italian history. New prosperity had come to the country and the standard of living had been raised.

But at the same time, the government had never solved the problem of unemployment. A large percentage of Italian workers remained out of work, even in the best of times, and during the economic slump that began to take serious hold in the early 1970s, the number of people out of work could be counted in the millions. Many of the unemployed were recent university graduates, who could find no jobs to suit the skills they had acquired in their education. Coupled with unemployment was inflation, which sometimes reached rates as high as 20 percent and made life difficult for those on small or moderate incomes.

Political corruption was the second problem that played into the hands of the Communists. By 1972, the Christian Democrats had been in power for twenty-five years—long enough for any party to grow fat and arrogant on its own success. In many parts of Italy, Christian Democrat politicians accepted bribes (often from anticommunist American corporations and from agencies of the United States government such as the CIA), dispensed patronage, and carelessly ignored the criticisms of their constituents. In contrast, the PCI was known and respected for its integrity and incorruptibility.

The third factor that contributed to the growing popularity of the Communist party was the rapid growth of political violence and terrorism, particularly after 1968. The violence and terror were the work of groups on the far left and far right who regarded Italian democracy as corrupt and worthless and wanted to bring it down. Bombings, kidnappings, assassinations, and other forms of assault—including the bizarre practice of shooting a victim's kneecaps so that he or she would be permanently disabled—became at that time an almost permanent part of Italian life.

The PCI prospered in this climate because it consistently condemned the political violence and terror and because the Communists offered an alternative to the problems of unemployment and inflation and political corruption. Many Italian voters had grown weary of the failure of the Christian Democrats to deal effectively with these problems and came to believe that some sort of change was necessary if Italian society was to survive.

The Historic Compromise. In 1968, the Italian Communist party condemned the Soviet invasion of Czechoslovakia that put down the moderate Communist regime of Alexander Dubcek. The Soviet invasion, the PCI declared, showed that the USSR was against national forms of communism—the idea that each country had the right to develop a form of Socialist government that best fit its own needs and circumstances. The Italian Communists promised to maintain their party's independence in spite of the Soviet action and to continue to support the independence of such Communist nations as Yugoslavia and Romania, both of which had developed policies often at odds with the Soviet Union.

Meanwhile, the political situation in Italy was still at an impasse. The Communists continued to improve in their strength at the polls, while the Christian Democrats failed to find a workable combination of parties to form a stable government. There was some movement in the left wing of the Christian Democrat party to create an "opening to the PCI" and include it within a new government, but this movement was not popular with Christian Democrat conservatives and moderates. The overall policy of the Social Democrats was still to exclude the Communists but to attempt to work with other parties of the left.

In 1973, Enrico Berlinguer, the head of the PCI, announced what he called the "Historic Compromise." Berlinguer is the descendant of an aristocratic Sardinian family and has made work in the Communist party his career. The Historic Compromise, he said, would be an alliance between the PCI and Italy's Catholic party, the Christian Democrats. This was the direction in which the Communists had been heading for several years, he added. No longer should the PCI be regarded as the party of "rupture" that stood against the government; it should now be considered as a constructive ally in building and improving Italian society.

Berlinguer explained that several reasons prompted him and his party to make the Historic Compromise. The first was a commitment to defending constitutional democracy, now threatened by Italy's economic crisis and the spread of terrorism. Communist cooperation with the Christian Democrats (and with the Socialists too if the Socialists wanted to come along) was essential for the future of democracy in Italy. Together, the major parties could establish stability and order. Opposed to one another, they would continue to create disorder and undermine the effectiveness of the government.

Berlinguer announced a second reason for the Historic Compromise after an analysis of the fate of a popularly elected leftist government in Chile. In 1970, he said, the Chilean people had chosen Dr. Salvadore Allende as President of their country in a three-way race. Allende received only 36.3 percent of the votes cast, but he proceeded to carry out a Socialist agenda that included the nationalization of American-owned businesses and other measures that deeply alienated the conservatives and moderates who had not voted for him.

In 1973, a coup d'état, led by anticommunist representatives of the military, brought the Socialist government down, and on the same day Allende died in the fighting—either a suicide or murder victim. The lesson for Italy in the story of Chilean socialism, Berlinguer said, was that no leftist government could come to power in a modern democracy without a *broad popular base*. He feared that communism in Italy would suffer a similar fate if it did not secure the respect and approval of the majority of the Italian people. And this respect and approval could only be won if the PCI proved that it could work well and smoothly with other parties in the Italian political system.

Over the next few years, the exact nature of the Historic Compromise emerged more clearly. In foreign affairs, the Communists showed their willingness to continue the policies already established by the Christian Democrats. Italy would still play a part in NATO—the Western European military alliance with the United States formed to protect against the possibility of Soviet aggression—and would maintain its economic ties with the nations of the West. At one point, Berlinguer stated that he felt more secure building communism in Italy under NATO than he would were Italy under the protection of the Soviet Union. The invasion of Czechoslovakia had dimmed his hopes that the USSR would permit the development of independent forms of Marxist societies within its sphere of influence. Independent communism could only thrive outside the limits of Soviet power.

In domestic affairs, the PCI continued to defend the constitutional system and individual rights. Communist leaders promised they would pay "rigorous fidelity to the concept of tolerance and respect for every human faith" and that "cultural expression must be protected absolutely." The PCI likewise announced that it preferred a "mixed economy," where private enterprise would continue to exist and play an important part in economic life. With the Historic Compromise and its policies, the Italian Communist party had adopted Eurocommunism.

Italian Elections after the Historic Compromise. In the years following the Historic Compromise, Communist popularity grew. Between 1972 and 1975, the percentage of Communist votes rose from 27.2 percent to almost 34 percent of the total votes cast for all parties, a gain of more than 6 percent. In the local and regional elections of June 1975, Communist candidates won control of many important cities and shared power with the Socialists and others in Venice, Naples, Florence, Milan, Verona, and Rome. In the same year, they came very close to receiving more votes than the Christian Democrats. It was the strongest showing the PCI had ever made.

In the national elections for the Italian legislature held in 1976, the Christian Democrats recovered somewhat, capturing 38.8 percent of the vote, but the Communists held their own, increasing slightly to 34.5 percent. The election proved the existence of a strong desire for reform in Italy and as a result, the new Christian Democrat leader, Giulio Andreotti, took steps to include the Communists informally and unofficially in the new government. No Communist was given a Cabinet-level post, but the Communists were able to exert some influence on legislation. Pietro Ingrao, a Communist, was named president of the Chamber of Deputies, while seven of twenty-six committee chairmanships, including posts in economic areas, went to Communist deputies. In exchange, the Communists were expected to support the Andreotti government by not bringing it down with a "no confidence" motion.

The Communists had come a long way since the exclusionary practices of 1947, but they were still not a full partner in the government. They now had one foot in the door, but the other foot remained outside. This situation bothered many PCI members, who believed the Communists had given too much and received too little. Communist party officials helped contribute to the stability of society by keeping down trade union demands for higher wages and by urging workers to avoid strikes that would cripple the economy. Yet these contributions to national order seemed to go unheeded by the Christian Democrats.

Early in 1978, Berlinguer began to demand a larger role in the government for the Communists. On nationwide television, he called for "a government of democratic solidarity" where Communists would hold Cabinet-level posts. But no meaningful compromise could be reached. One year later, in 1979, Berlinguer and the Communists in the Italian parliament voted to bring down the Andreotti government, complaining that the Christian Democrats had failed to carry through needed economic and social reforms and had failed to recognize the right of the PCI to share power.

When elections for the national legislature were held in June of that year, however, the PCI suffered its first loss in popularity in more than thirty years. The Communists received 31.4 percent of the vote, a loss of 2.4 percent since 1976. The Christian Democrats received 38.5 percent, down 0.4 percent. Other parties remained much the same, while four small parties of the middle and far left increased slightly.

What had happened to cause the decline in support for the Communists? Several factors were probably to blame. Italian voters, some observers argued, had not been convinced by the party's liberal Eurocommunist line and perhaps suspected that at heart all Communists remained Stalinists. Other observers said that the decline in support for both major parties may indicate voter weariness with both the Christian Democrats and the Communist party and a decision to look elsewhere for political alternatives.

However, whatever the reason, the Communist loss was too small to mean much in the complex world of Italian politics. The Christian Democrats were still a minority party that would have to search for partners to govern effectively and the Communists were still a strong, well-organized unit that could continue to demand its right to play a role in the government.

In short, Italian political life would continue to be much the same as it had been for more than twenty years.

The Communist loss was also too small to spell doom for the doctrine of Eurocommunism. Throughout the election campaign, Berlinguer defended the positions he had taken under the Historic Compromise. He attacked the Soviet Union for its concentration camps and its persecution of dissidents and continued to defend constitutional democracy. He maintained the independence of the PCI and its right to pursue its own course toward communism. Only the future will tell if Eurocommunism will help to restore the losses suffered by the PCI in the elections of 1979 and to bring the PCI into full participation in the government.

CHAPTER SIX

EUROCOMMUNISM IN FRANCE

The second largest Communist party in Western Europe is the French Communist party, or PCF. With an estimated 600,000 members, it is roughly one-third the size of the Italian party but nevertheless plays an important role in French political life. Like its Italian counterpart, the PCF controls trade unions, has its own youth groups, and runs a publishing house which regularly turns out numerous books and pamphlets supporting the Communist movement. One out of every five French voters—or 20 percent of the electorate—has supported the Communist party in recent elections and more than seventy major cities have Communist or a combination of Communist and Socialist administrations.

The Origins of the Party. The French Communist party was founded in 1920, and like most Communist parties established in the years following the Russian Revolution, it patterned itself on the party of the Soviet Union. Iron discipline and submission to authority were expected of all party members. The

early PCF was a small but dedicated group. It joined the Communist International (Comintern) and worked within France to spread the Communist message to factory workers and other members of the proletariat.

The French Communist party first began to play an influential role in French society during the political crisis of the 1930s. Hitler's rise to power in Germany had created a great deal of concern among moderates and leftists in many European countries. Italy had had a Fascist government since 1922 and now Germany, too, had fallen victim to a party of the extreme right. Fascism seemed the wave of the future and threatened to topple the European democracies one by one.

In order to diminish the threat of fascism in France, Maurice Thorez (1900–1964), a former factory worker who had risen in the party ranks to become head of the PCF, proposed the idea of a Popular Front. The Popular Front would be a union of Communists, Socialists, liberals, and other antifascists organized under a common commitment to preserve the democratic system and protect individual liberties. Thorez, along with Palmiro Togliatti, the Italian Communist then in exile from his country, and Georgi Dimitrov, the Comintern's representative in Western Europe, set out to persuade Stalin that the Popular Front deserved his support. The Soviet leader, who saw the Popular Front as a means of winning friends and allies in the West and strengthening the USSR in case of a German invasion, was easily won over.

In 1936, the Popular Front—composed of the Communists, Socialists, and middle-class democrats—won an impressive victory. The French Socialist party won the largest number of votes and its leader, Leon Blum, became Premier of France.

Maurice Thorez, a former factory worker who rose to become head of the PCF.

But Communist participation in the Front—even though the Communists had refused to accept Cabinet posts—angered conservative opinion in France, and the Communists themselves grew disillusioned with Blum's timid policies. All this led eventually to the downfall of Blum's government after only two years. The failure of the Popular Front revealed the difficulty of uniting political parties with different philosophies. Yet the Front did establish a tradition of Communist cooperation in the democratic system of France, a tradition the PCF was never to abandon.

World War II and Following. During World War II, northern France was occupied by the Nazis, while a Fascist government was established in the south. The Communist party at that time went underground and became one of the leading organizers of the resistance movement. Communists fought German soldiers and sabotaged Nazi military installations. Many party members were imprisoned and executed or lost their lives in combat. At the end of the war, the Communists emerged with a reputation for courage and patriotism which gained them widespread respect throughout the country.

The PCF had won 14.76 percent of the vote in the Popular Front elections of 1936. Ten years later, in 1946, it achieved 28.2 percent, the highest it has yet attained. Communists played an important part in the government and shared political power with other parties. Maurice Thorez, the party leader, declared that the way to communism "is necessarily different from the Russian way in every country." This was an early declaration in support of an independent form of communism in France, a form that would emerge more fully over the next two decades. Unlike the Italian party, however, which grew rapidly after the war, the PCF opted for a smaller membership in the hope that a smaller party could be better organized than a larger one.

The advent of the Cold War brought a momentary end

to Communist ambitions in France. Conservative, moderate, and Socialist politicians, backed by the power and influence of the United States, established a government under the leadership of the Socialist Paul Ramadier that excluded the Communists. Communist influence in the French trade union movement was likewise weakened by the creation of a separate group of unions, free of Communist control.

The PCF and De-Stalinization. Khrushchev's denunciation of Stalin at the 20th Party Congress in 1956 hurt the French Communist party severely. A period of debate and soul-searching followed, as the party membership divided between hardline Stalinists—who formed a majority of the party's ranks—and the minority, which was willing to accept de-Stalinization and innovation. In 1961, Thorez declared that the PCF would never apply the Soviet model of communism to France and two years later he added that "The theory of the single [party] in a Communist regime is an error of Stalin's." In 1964 and 1967, the 17th and 18th Congresses of the PCF likewise rejected the notion of the single-party state.

Taken together, these moves indicated that French communism had abandoned Stalinism in favor of innovation and planned to work within the parliamentary system. What remained to be done was the creation of a coalition with another party or parties. In 1958, General Charles de Gaulle, the great French hero of World War II, had been elected head of the government in a landslide. In the election, the PCF had received the lowest number of votes it was to receive in any postwar election. Obviously, if the Communists were to stage a comeback and play an influential role in French politics, it would be best to do so in conjunction with another party.

The obvious choice for a political partner was one of France's leftist parties. Since 1934, the year the Popular Front was first suggested, there had been a history of cooperation between the PCF and French Socialists. In the 1950s, Thorez' successor as head of the party, Waldeck Rochet, had forged an election alliance with the Socialists. The Socialist party had fallen into disarray in the 1960s, but the Communists were able to reach an agreement with Francois Mitterrand, a man with Socialist connections, and they supported his bid for the Presidency in 1965.

Mitterrand received 44.8 percent of the vote in a close run-off election with President de Gaulle. It was an excellent showing that revealed the power of the left in France when the leftist parties worked together. Two years later, in 1967, the PCF reached a second agreement with parties of the left during elections for the National Assembly. The Communists promised to let their candidates step aside in support of a leftist candidate from another party if the noncommunist leftist candidate received the larger vote in the first election. In return, the other leftist parties promised to throw their support to the Communist candidate if he or she received the larger number of votes in the first election.*

This agreement was reached without complete accord between the parties involved on policy matters. The Communists maintained their own platform, while other parties maintained theirs. In the presidential election of 1969, this lack of accord on policy led the two principal parties of the left to run two separate candidates, both of whom lost in the first election to Georges Pompidou, de Gaulle's successor. Working together, the left had achieved a near victory with Mitterrand in 1965; working separately, it had lost decisively.

The Union of the Left and the Common Platform. The year 1968 was an important one for the PCF. In May, a rebellion begun by students and other young people of the New Left

* This agreement was reached because of the peculiar rules governing French elections. If no candidate receives a majority of votes in the first round of a French election, a runoff is held so that voters can choose between the two candidates who have received the largest number of votes.

was joined by French workers and for a while France was in turmoil. The Communist party did not support the rebellion. Instead, it worked to separate the workers and the students and thereby defuse the power of the rebellion. At Communist urging, the government granted the workers higher wages and better benefits and by early summer, the crisis had passed. The PCF had shown that it preferred national stability to upheaval and that it was willing to work to preserve democracy rather than take advantage of a crisis to destroy it. In 1968, too, as further proof of its independence, the French Communist party condemned the Soviet invasion of Czechoslovakia and issued its "Champigny Manifesto" calling for the establishment of "advanced democracy" in France. At the same time, negotiations were begun that culminated three and a half years later in a new agreement with a newly reorganized French Socialist party.

This agreement—announced in 1972—was known as the "Union of the Left" and had been ardently sought by the leader of the French Communist party, Georges Marchais. The Union of the Left issued a joint "Common Platform" that elaborated the plans of the Communists and Socialists, should they be elected to power. The platform proposed to end "the injustice and the incoherence of the present regime" and went on to list an agenda of reform that included the nationalization of a number of corporations, banks, and industries. The Union of the Left was not a merger of the two parties and each party reserved the right to criticize the policies and actions of the other. But the Union was an understanding that the left could work together on general terms.

In order to spell out the role of the Communist party in the Union of the Left and in French political life, Georges Marchais authored a book entitled *The Democratic Challenge*, which was published in August 1973 by a noncommunist press. The book was intended to quiet the fears and distrust of moderates and others who believed that the PCF was a totalitarian party that advocated Soviet-style communism. The book was an immediate success and sold more than 700,000 copies by the end of the year.

In *The Democratic Challenge,* Marchais assured his readers of the Communist commitment to the democratic system. The Soviet Union, he wrote, offers no model for France to follow. Any government that the Communist party would join would remain French and would have total respect for French traditions, including freedom of the press and freedom to worship as one saw fit. Catholics and Communists, he insisted, could and should learn to work together in areas of mutual concern. Together they could reach solutions that would solve the social and economic problems facing the country.

Marchais claimed that the target of the Communist party was the super-rich, the huge corporations and banks and other organizations that exploited every class of people. The PCF stood ready to defend not only the worker, but also the interests of the middle class. The Communists did not seek the nationalization of small factories, businesses, or farms; these would remain in the private sector. Communism meant simply an extension of democracy to include all elements of society.

Instead of the present situation, where all decisions came from the wealthy and powerful few, the PCF advocated a system where the views and opinions of everyone counted. The French Communist party, Marchais said, was above all else a patriotic party that sought what was best for France. In foreign policy and in domestic affairs, it would strive to maintain complete independence from foreign influence, whether that influence came from giant corporations, the American government, or the Soviet Union.

In the parliamentary elections of 1973, the Union of the Left scored nearly as many votes as the coalition of parties that were in the government. It was a hopeful comeback from the decline of earlier years. In the presidential elections held the next year, the Union ran the Socialist François Mitterrand against the candidate of the moderate parties, Valery Giscard d'Estaing. Mitterrand nearly carried the election.

To promote its ideas and gain popularity and influence, the PCF began a public relations campaign in the months after the presidential election. Marchais appeared before open party meetings in village halls and community auditoriums. Noncommunist journalists were allowed to question and examine party policy and practice, and party leaders answered questions before critical audiences throughout France. The purpose of the public relations campaign was to convince French voters of the openness and flexibility of the party and of its willingness to play the democratic game just as other parties played it.

At the same time, Communist party leaders launched a series of critical attacks on the Socialists, accusing them of timidity, lack of Marxist commitment, and a willingness to abandon their Communist allies once the Union of the Left had achieved power. The attacks grew quite bitter on occasion, yet they were designed not to destroy the Union or the Common Platform but to placate hardline Communists in the PCF—the men and women who had never been pleased with Communist cooperation with other parties. The attacks were meant to show the hardliners that the party still stood alone and had not "sold out" to the Socialists.

The PCF and the Dictatorship of the Proletariat. In 1975, the Communists stopped their criticism of the Socialists and turned once again toward strengthening and improving the Union of the Left. Marchais offered renewed pledges of his party's desire for democracy and peaceful change. In November, he made a trip to Rome to visit with the leader of the Italian

Communist party, Enrico Berlinguer, in order to show his support for Berlinguer's policies and the Historic Compromise of the Italian party.

Indeed, Marchais' brand of communism had come to sound very much like the Historic Compromise of the PCI. Like Berlinguer, Marchais had come to the conclusion that the best policy for the Communist parties of the West was to do everything possible to extend democracy and make it work. "[The French should be] doing everything, doing absolutely everything," Marchais was once quoted as saying, "to enlarge to the limit the alliance of political and social forces which, seeking a renovating policy of democracy and national independence, support a program of clearly defined democratic reforms."

In line with its commitment to democracy, the PCF declared its repudiation of "the dictatorship of the proletariat." Many European political observers regarded this step as genuine proof that real change was afoot in the French Communist party. The dictatorship of the proletariat, after all, was an idea discussed by Marx and developed in a particular Russian context under Lenin and Stalin. It implied the necessity of a dictatorship following a Communist revolution, a dictatorship that would root out the old order and make way for the new. It formed a central part of the theory and practice of Marxism-Leninism and was still defended by Moscow. Its rejection by the French Communists, these observers concluded, could only mean that the PCF had abandoned the Soviet doctrine of violent revolution and the use of force, in support of a more moderate path to communism.

Marchais' visit to Berlinguer in Rome and his party's rejection of the dictatorship of the proletariat were dramatic demonstrations of the French Communists' flexibility and willingness to be innovative. In the parliamentary elections of 1976, the policy apparently paid off. The Socialists and Communists, working together, managed to increase the number of their delegates in the National Assembly. But both parties pinned their greatest hopes on the presidential elections scheduled for March 1978. The prestige of the Union of the Left seemed to be on the rise, while the popularity of President Giscard d'Estaing was waning. Inflation and unemployment plagued the economy and caused many voters to desire a change of administration. Polls showed that the left had a very good chance of winning and that Mitterrand might well be the next President of France, the head of a Socialist-Communist coalition elected by a majority of French voters.

The Common Platform of 1972 was revised to reflect the new needs and problems of the nation. It called for the nationalization of French industries involving armaments, aeronautics and space, nuclear energy, pharmaceuticals, electronics, mineral resources, chemicals, and computers. Banks, oil companies, and the steel and car industries were likewise considered as areas where government control and supervision were needed, but the Communists and Socialists disagreed on how far and how quickly the government should move into these sectors.

For the worker, the Common Platform raised the minimum wage, a step needed in a country where the cost of living was high but the average wage relatively low. It likewise called for the standardization of the working week at forty hours. The Socialists opposed a Communist move to make the highest wages in France no more than five times the lowest. The Socialists feared that this and other similar recommendations of the PCF might be too extreme for many French voters and cause them to vote for more moderate politicians.

Indeed, the Common Platform for the elections of 1978 was worked out only after a period of disagreement between the PCF and the Socialists that sometimes grew quite bitter. Six months before the election, the two parties seemed to have dissolved the Union, only to reach a reconciliation sometime later. The frequent arguing led some observers unfriendly to the left to point out that two parties that got along so poorly before an election would most certainly find it hard to govern together harmoniously and peacefully once they had been elected to office.

Polls taken a short time before the election showed the leftist Union winning by a margin of 7 percent. When the final votes were counted, however, the left had lost—a loss all the more resounding because victory had seemed so close. The Socialists received only 22.6 percent of the vote—they had hoped for at least 30 percent. The PCF received 20.6 percent—no more than they had received in many previous elections. The parties of the right—the conservatives and moderates—carried the election and Valery Giscard d'Estaing remained in office.

What had happened to crush the hopes of the French left? The Socialists and Communists blamed each other for the defeat—the Communists claiming that the Socialists had been too timid, the Socialists charging that the Communists appeared too militant and radical. Conservative and moderate observers traced the leftist loss to the "natural conservatism" of the French voter. The average French citizen, they said, might vote Communist as a means of protest. When it came down to the final test, however, he or she would vote for a more moderate candidate or even a conservative candidate, because few people really wanted the changes promised by the Common Platform.

What the fate of Eurocommunism in France will be is unclear at this time. One party intellectual, analyzing the reasons for the defeat of 1978, has said that the PCF must now prove its commitment to the doctrines of Eurocommunism or face even greater losses in elections to come. Georges Marchais and other party officials have renewed their commitment from time to time. At the same time, however, journalists have recorded some talk that the PCF will adopt a more strict Communist line at its next party congress, a line that will be a step away from Eurocommunism and a step toward reconciliation with Moscow and Soviet-style communism.

CHAPTER SEVEN

EUROCOMMUNISM IN SPAIN

The Spanish Communist party (PCE) is small compared to the large and impressive Italian Communist party and the Communist party of France. It has rarely had the chance to play a significant role in Spanish society and was only recently legalized after almost forty years of clandestine existence. Yet most experts on Eurocommunism agree that the PCE and its leader, Santiago Carrillo, are the heart and soul of the Euro-communist movement. The Italian and French parties have worked to establish their commitment to democracy and their independence from Moscow, but the PCE has been the leader in the search for a communism that is free of totalitarianism and all traces of Stalinism.

The Early Years. The PCE has had a difficult and tempestuous history. Founded in 1921, it remained small in numbers and confined for the most part to a few large cities for more than a decade. However, in 1931 a mild revolution forced King Alfonso XIII from his throne and brought about the creation of a democratic Spanish republic. The Communists were able to play an active part in the political ferment and upheaval that followed. Spanish liberals and leftists wanted to preserve the precarious republic, but they were opposed by the right wing—a strong and often violent force in Spanish life—which had never accepted the idea of democracy and desired a return to the old order.

After 1933, the Spanish government fell increasingly into the hands of conservatives who attempted to put a stop to all reform. The parties of the left banded together to form a Popular Front which included moderate Republicans, Socialists (who formed the single largest party), and Communists. The Popular Front won a victory in the elections of February 1936, sending 267 deputies to the National Assembly, to the right's 132. The election, however, settled nothing and the right-wing parties refused to abide by their defeat. In July, a number of army generals began an insurrection against the government and soon all of Spain fell into a bitter and protracted civil war.

The Spanish right, a collection of conservatives, Fascists, militarists, and Monarchists with the support of the Roman Catholic Church, received aid from Hitler and Mussolini, the leaders of Germany and Italy. The left depended for the most part on the support of the Soviet Union and Communists throughout the world. Stalin sent money and supplies, while Communists and other leftists from the United States, Great Britain, France, and several other Western nations formed the International Brigades to fight for the Spanish republic. The Spanish Civil War was bloody and destructive and was characterized by atrocities and extreme cruelties committed by both sides. The war left an indelible image on everyone who lived through it and is remembered to this day with anguish and sorrow by Spanish leftists, who were defeated in 1939.

One of the rebel soldiers, General Franco, emerged as absolute leader and dictator of the country. All political parties except his own—the National Movement—were outlawed. Between 1939 and 1942, Franco imprisoned nearly two million men and women who failed to support him and executed an estimated 200,000. "We do not believe in government through the voting booth," the General declared. "The Spanish national will was never freely expressed through the ballot box. Spain has no foolish dreams."

Franco's campaign against his political enemies devastated the Spanish Communist party. During the Civil War, party membership had risen because of the wholehearted Communist support for the republican cause. Now, the Communists who survived imprisonment or execution went underground where the party continued a precarious and illegal existence. Others, like the Civil War heroine Delores Ibarruri, better known as La Passionaria (The Passionate One), went into exile, many to the Soviet Union. Santiago Carrillo, the present leader of the party, escaped during the last days of the war.

For the next thirty-six years, until his death in 1975, Franco continued his one-man, one-party rule. He exercised severe censorship over the press and established a secret police to root out all dissent. His regime was characterized by a stern religiosity and devout Catholicism that permeated all aspects of Spanish life. During World War II, Spain remained neutral, but nevertheless sent a crack army division to fight alongside the Nazis against the Soviet Union. After the war, the reputation of the country was so bad that for several years the United Nations and later the European Common Market refused it permission to join their organizations.

The Party in Exile. After World War II, the PCE established its headquarters in Paris where Carrillo and a number of other leading Spanish Communists had made their homes. Party activity in Spain was limited to a small guerrilla war in the Pyrenees, directed against the Franco dictatorship. It

was a hopeless and futile cause and, in 1948, after meeting in Moscow with Stalin, Carrillo and Ibarruri decided that other steps had to be taken. On Stalin's advice, they put an end to the guerrilla war and ordered party members to begin the infiltration of Spain's trade unions. The decision was one of the wisest moves the PCE made during its clandestine years. By working with the unions, the party gained a base of popular support it had lost after the Civil War and began to pave the way for a more active role in Spanish life at a later time.

In 1956, the PCE, from its Paris headquarters, launched its plan for "national reconciliation." The plan was designed to build a broad anti-Franco coalition of moderates and leftists in Spain. The PCE likewise supported Khrushchev's de-Stalinization movement, but stopped short of the soul-searching and change that were beginning to take place in the French and Italian parties. At this time, Carrillo supported the Soviet invasion of Hungary and defended Soviet society as a model for all Communist parties to follow.

Indeed, Carrillo's approval of the Soviet Union continued for several years—a fact that has made his opponents suspicious of his true acceptance of Eurocommunism. As late as 1964, Carrillo was using his power as head of the Spanish party—a post he received in 1959—to root out party members who disagreed with his hardline communism. At a PCE executive committee meeting in Prague, he declared, "For us it is clear that Marxism-Leninism is one, and that there is not a distinct Marxism-Leninism for the Chinese, the Russians, the Spaniards, the French, and the Italians. For us it is clear that proletarian internationalism is and should be the rule of our conduct. We will defend Marxism-Leninism, the unity of

Generalissimo Francisco Franco
(1892–1975)

the Communist movement at one with the Soviet Communist party."

The events of 1968, however, forever undermined Carrillo's faith in the Soviet Union. For some time, he had been working on an alliance with moderate opponents of Franco in Spain, a continuation of the goal of national reconciliation begun in 1956. Part of the success depended on Carrillo's convincing his potential allies that the PCE respected democracy and would abide by democratic rules. To prove its independence from Soviet domination and its willingness to innovate, the PCE supported the regime of Alexander Dubcek in Czechoslovakia, where Dubcek was attempting to create a more open Communist society, guarantee individual liberties, and abolish Soviet-style totalitarianism.

When the Soviet Union, along with soldiers from other Eastern European countries, invaded Czechoslovakia, Carrillo was horrified. The experiment in moderate communism he had held up as an example of proof that communism could be democratic was destroyed and replaced by a government subservient to the Soviet Union. Delores Ibarruri, La Passionaria, presented a formal protest from the PCE to the Kremlin and Carrillo joined Enrico Berlinguer of Italy and Georges Marchais of France in condemning the Soviet action. Carrillo's connection with Soviet communism had been severed, and in the years that followed, he began to move toward the positions that have made him widely known as the chief theoretician of Eurocommunism.

The Return to Spain. In 1974 the PCE's hopes for a broad anti-Franco force were realized when the Communists joined the Junta Democratica, a union of Spanish moderates and liberals opposed to Franco's rule. Carrillo explained that the purpose of the Junta was to establish an alliance of "democratic forces" that could help guide Spain to genuine democracy once Franco had died. The Junta, he added, was open to the entire "civilized right, including monarchists, bankers, and big industrialists."

On November 20, 1975, General Franco died at the age of eighty-two. Power passed with relative ease to Franco's chosen successor, King Juan Carlos, who proceeded to follow a policy of slow and deliberate reform—slow so that he would not alienate the extreme right, which still remained strongly Francoist, but deliberate so that the moderate and leftist parties would be satisfied that things would not remain the same.

The first sign that the King planned to dismantle the dictatorship came early in 1976 when he appointed a moderate, Adolfo Suarez Gonzalez, to be head of the government. Suarez proceeded to dissolve Franco's old party, the National Movement, and to announce a partial amnesty for nearly a thousand prisoners who had been imprisoned for their political activities and beliefs. The amnesty included many Communists, two of whom were leading officials in the party hierarchy.

Carrillo returned secretly to Spain in February and remained in the background until December, when he held a press conference in Madrid. He was arrested twelve days later, held for eight days, and then released on bond, a sure sign that the restrictive police actions of Franco's era were a thing of the past. During the next few months, Carrillo worked for the legalization of the Communist party by portraying himself as a democrat who supported national unity and harmony. He disowned his Stalinist past and emphasized his party's connections with the Communist parties of France and Italy by calling for a "Eurocommunist Summit" that brought Berlinguer and Marchais to Madrid in support of Carrillo in March 1977.

One month later, Prime Minister Suarez legalized the PCE. Talk of a military coup d'état spread throughout Spain after the announcement was officially made. But after a meeting of the Supreme Council of the Armed Forces, the generals agreed to follow the orders of the government "for patriotism's sake." They did not like the decision, they said, but they would abide by it. Indeed, the generals probably had little choice. If they had attempted to stop the legalization of the PCE, leftists of all parties would have taken to the streets to demonstrate and protest. Spain would have been plunged into a crisis similar to the crisis that developed into the Spanish Civil War in 1936.

With legalization, the PCE began its move to become part of the mainstream of Spanish life. In its first legal meeting on Spanish soil in thirty-eight years, the 152-member Central Committee heard Santiago Carrillo promise that the Communists would "abide by the rules of the democratic game." The path to Spanish democracy is narrow, he went on, and the PCE must be moderate in its demands or risk provoking its many enemies.

The legalization of the PCE also came in time for its participation in the first free elections to be held in Spain since 1936. Prime Minister Suarez set the date for the elections as June 15, 1977, and invited the entire spectrum of Spanish politics, from right to left, to participate. The Communists joined in, fielding candidates for a wide variety of offices and hoping to capture at least 12 percent of the vote.

"Spain will surprise you," Suarez had said when pessimists predicted that democracy would never work in Spain. When the results of the election were announced, they showed a victory for the moderate policies of the new government and a rejection of extremes, whether of the far left or far right. The conservatives—who called themselves the Popular Alliance—received only 8.2 percent of the vote, while the Democratic Center Union—which supported Suarez—received 34 percent. The Socialist Worker's party took 28.5 percent and the PCE only 9 percent, winning twenty seats in the 350-seat Congress of Deputies.

However, Carrillo expressed no disappointment at his party's failure to capture the 12 percent it had hoped for. The Communists, he insisted, had been successful in other ways. They had shown themselves to be a moderate, patriotic party, concerned about Spain's democratic future. In addition, the PCE had made a large step toward the recognition it lacked as a result of almost forty years of illegality.

Nor did the PCE's relatively weak showing cause Carrillo to abandon his Eurocommunist policies or play them down in any way. In April 1978, the party endorsed a proposal to drop its "Leninist" label and adopt the more moderate sounding "Marxist, Democratic, and Revolutionary." The change was significant for two reasons. First, it indicated that the PCE, like the other Eurocommunist parties, had dropped the idea of a Leninist-style seizure of power. And second, it was significant because the change in label was agreed upon by an unusually open party conference, where debate was public. The Spanish Communist party, unlike any other Communist party, had reached a decision democratically within the structure of the party itself. Many decisions were still made by the party hierarchy behind closed doors, but now the PCE seemed more like other political parties—divided and factional, yet willing to reach a final decision on policy through debate and general consensus.

Eurocommunism and the State. Carrillo has been quite open about what he wants Eurocommunism to achieve. In his many speeches in Spain, in his book *Eurocommunism and the State,* and on his lecture tour of American universities, he elaborated his ideas. "Eurocommunism must show that the victory of the Socialist forces in Western Europe will not multiply Soviet power nor presuppose the extension of the one-party Soviet model," he writes. "Eurocommunism must be an independent experience with a more advanced socialism that will have a positive influence on the democratic evolution [of other societies]."

In short, Carrillo accepts democracy because he sees the democratic system as offering the best means toward the creation of "a more advanced socialism" that will avoid the inequalities and totalitarianism of Soviet-style communism. Democracy can avoid the pitfalls of Stalinism and one-person rule. It allows the expression of everyone's opinion so that a consensus can be reached on public policy. But democracy must be full and complete and extended to the furthest degree possible. Only then can a nation evolve into a truly just and egalitarian communism.

Carrillo warns that Eurocommunism does not completely rule out the use of force. If the dominant classes, he says, were to close off democratic channels and the circumstances that make revolution possible, then the Communist party would find it necessary to use force to reestablish democracy and give the lower classes a voice in affairs. Above all, he insists, don't think of Eurocommunism as social democracy or that the Eurocommunists have given up the final goals of Marxism. "We want to transform capitalist society," he reminds us, "not manage it."

For Spain, Carrillo believes that democracy is essential and must be firmly established. "The Spanish people," he has said from time to time, "do not want another Civil War. And our party takes that into account." The PCE will not lead the Spanish nation from a Franco-style dictatorship into a Stalinist totalitarianism. Carrillo is proud of his party's commitment to democracy in Spain and proud of the changes in party rules that have made the party itself more democratic. Never again one line of thought for Spanish Communists, he promised a meeting of his Central Committee. "There will be a free confrontation among responsible militants of the party, and it will be much more free and much more open the more we are decided to reinforce and keep united."

Carrillo and the PCE will have a difficult time for several years to come. Many Spanish leftists find Communist party policies too moderate and believe that Carrillo has gone too far in his support of the present system in Spain. At the same time, many moderates and conservatives still regard the Communists with a great deal of distrust and misgiving. Spain itself suffers from unemployment, inflation, and a terrorist movement responsible for the deaths of a number of high political and military officials. But Carrillo offers stability to Spain and stability is what Spain needs at the present time. If the party is able to continue its difficult and precarious course between the right and the left, it may well emerge as one of the most interesting political experiments of recent times—a Marxist party that avoids the mistakes of the Soviet Union yet remains true to the basic ideals of communism.

CHAPTER EIGHT

THE DILEMMA
OF EUROCOMMUNISM

In recent years, the doctrines of Eurocommunism have added new strength and vitality to the Communist parties of Italy, France, and Spain. Communism has scored many electoral successes and has made a place for itself in the political mainstream of those three countries. But nowhere has Eurocommunism led to the participation of Communist party members in the highest levels of government. An invisible line seems to separate the party from its present situation and the final victory at the polls that would give it the national power it seeks. What reasons can explain this failure to achieve a final victory? The answer to the dilemma may be simple and uncomplicated. In spite of its popularity, Eurocommunism is still too new to be trusted by the masses of voters. The electorate has yet to be convinced that its commitment to democracy is genuine, and the Stalinist past of the Communist movement is too fresh in everyone's memory for widespread acceptance of the fact that communism has acquired a new face.

Many conservatives and moderates doubt the sincerity of

the Eurocommunists and believe that all communism, at bottom, remains totalitarian and antidemocratic. Most of this criticism has come from expected quarters: from business people who fear Communist plans for economic change, from religious leaders who distrust Communist atheism, and from men and women concerned with national security who believe that Eurocommunism may strengthen the Soviet Union's presence in Western Europe. In spite of the massive Eurocommunist effort to assure the voters of Italy, France, and Spain of their party's patriotism and desire for stability, these critics remain unconvinced.

But Eurocommunism has also aroused a great deal of mistrust and doubt among people who would seem to have every reason to welcome its appearance. Socialists and other leftist parties have added their criticisms to the denunciations offered by conservatives and moderates, and in many cases their criticisms have been among the most severe that Eurocommunism has experienced. For the most part, these criticisms come from three main sources: the established and successful moderate Socialist parties of northern Europe, from parties of the extreme left, and from intellectuals.

The Socialist Criticism. These critics come for the most part from countries where Socialist parties are strong and the Communist parties small and weak. At a meeting in Denmark held in February 1976, Socialist leaders from Great Britain, Germany, Denmark, Sweden, and Austria firmly rejected any compromise with Eurocommunism. "We see no reason to engage in any kind of cooperation," said Helmut Schmidt, the Chancellor of West Germany. Any sort of cooperation with the Communists of Italy, France, or Spain, he added, would endanger NATO and damage the economies of Western European nations. What the Socialist leaders seemed to imply was that Eurocommunism offered no new alternative.

It was the same old Soviet-style communism in slightly altered form to make it more attractive.

Criticism from the Far Left. To the men and women of the far left, Eurocommunism appears as a watered-down version of communism, a rejection of the revolutionary past, and a compromise with the enemy, middle-class liberalism. The members of Italy's Red Brigade—a terrorist group responsible for many recent violent acts against prominent Italian citizens—say the PCI has become too conservative and too concerned with the preservation of its position in Italian political life to make a commitment to genuine Communist change. In addition, the decline of support for the Communist party in the elections of 1979 and the growth in the number of votes for two parties of the far left in Italy, reveals that the PCI has lost some of its militant support to hardline revolutionary parties.

Carrillo and the Spanish Communist party have come under similar attacks. In 1977 a leading Spanish Marxist scholar denounced Carrillo's tactics in a Communist journal. "Eurocommunism," he wrote, "to the extent that one can take it seriously, is not a strategy toward socialism. It is, on the contrary, the latest retreat reached by the real Communist movement." The significance of such attacks is that they undermine Eurocommunism from the left at a time when the Eurocommunists are attempting to convince the right of their integrity and sincerity. As a result, the Communist parties of the West appear to be confused and disoriented and to have no genuine commitment in any direction.

Criticism from the Intellectuals. Some of the most bitter attacks on Eurocommunism—and on communism of any kind—come from a small group of French writers known as the "new philosophers." These writers had at one time been members of leftist organizations and had taken part in the events of May 1968, when student rebels and their allies from the working class went to the streets in protest against the policies of the French government. In recent years, however, their leftist sympathies have waned and they have become highly critical of many of their earlier political views.

The new philosophers have turned out at least fourteen books—several have been bestsellers—that denounce communism and warn their readers that communism, in any form, should be regarded as an enemy of human freedom and dignity. Bernard-Henri Levy, perhaps the best known of the group, calls communism "barbarism with a human face." Leftists delude themselves into believing a just and humane Communist society can be established. Communism, by its very nature, Levy claims, is harsh, uncompromising, and totalitarian.

Levy likewise warns that the idea of revolution is a myth. Revolution does not bring change or improvement; it more than likely brings chaos, bloodshed, and widespread unhappiness. The great writer of our time, Levy says, is the Russian Alexander Solzhenitsyn, a writer who has shown his readers the true face of communism. Read Solzhenitsyn, Levy seems to imply, and you will never again be seduced by the claims of Marxism.

André Glucksmann, another of the new philosophers and a former Communist, condemns any system that claims to be a "human science." These systems—and communism is one of them—pretend to know the answers for all of humankind's problems, but in reality they are not sciences, merely someone's opinion. In actual fact, these pseudo-sciences lead to totalitarianism and to the manipulation of human beings by an all-powerful government. Glucksmann believes that one of the tragedies of our time is the existence of a number of philosophies, like Marxism, which try to force all humankind into a given framework.

But the writer who has been responsible for the most

widely read attacks on communism and Eurocommunism is the journalist and social critic Jean-François Revel. Revel, who is a generation older than the group known as the "new philosophers," describes himself as "a man of the left." He put forth his criticisms of communism in a book entitled *The Totalitarian Temptation*. Stalinism, he wrote, is the essence of communism. Brezhnev, the present leader of the Soviet Union, and the Italian Eurocommunist Enrico Berlinguer differ little from the former Soviet dictator. They may be less bloodthirsty and not as strict in their application of Communist principles, but in the end they are equally as antidemocratic and intolerant as Stalin. The essential thrust of communism is always toward greater monopoly and power, not toward freedom and individual rights.

Revel claims that we should not be taken in by Eurocommunism's conversion to democracy. In the past other Communists have announced their devotion to democracy. Georgi Dimitrov, the Bulgarian Communist, promised that "Bulgaria will not be a Soviet republic, but a people's republic. There will be no dictatorship." But dictatorship did indeed follow. Matyas Rakosi, the Hungarian Stalinist, argued publicly that there were several paths to communism and then proceeded to govern Hungary in slavish imitation of the Soviet Union. If Communist leaders have lied in the past in order to disguise their true aims, why should we believe the Eurocommunists now?

We do not know how the Eurocommunists would wield power if they were elected to office, Revel points out, because they have never been in national power. But one thing is certain. There is no reason to believe that they would grant to the nation at large the same rights they deny their own party members. The Italian and French parties are still closed, strictly Leninist organizations, Revel claims, that discourage debate and criticism. They expect total obedience from party members and total acceptance of the doctrines handed down by the party leadership. If the Eurocommunist leaders are accustomed to this sort of submissiveness from party members, Revel asks, what would they expect from the public at large?

But Revel reserves some of his most biting criticism for the Common Platform, the statement of purpose put forth by the Union of the Left. The Common Platform, he says, was a fraud. The Communists entered into the Union with the Socialists only because they believed they could control and dominate the Socialist party. There was no genuine agreement of principles, simply a cynical manipulation of the Union to advance Communist interests. The Socialists, blinded by their own desire for power, could not see that they were being used and deceived themselves into believing that the Communists could be controlled. The Common Platform, Revel believes, would have been political suicide for France.

The Attitudes of the Superpowers. The Eurocommunists have failed to convince a sizable portion of public opinion that their commitment to democracy and their independence of the Soviet Union are genuine. But the dilemma and difficulties facing the ultimate success of the Eurocommunist movement do not end there. The Eurocommunists also lack the support of the world's two major powers, the Soviet Union and the United States. Both superpowers have a strong interest in what takes place in Europe and both have kept a watchful eye on the progress of Eurocommunism.

At first glance, it would seem that the Soviet Union would welcome the success of the Western European Communists. But this has not been so. At best, the USSR has taken an ambivalent attitude toward the movement, sometimes praising its victories, but at other times mildly chastising it for infractions of Soviet policy. At worst, Moscow has condemned the Western Communists in terms usually reserved for Communist renegades such as Mao Tse-tung of China and Tito of Yugoslavia. Santiago Carrillo, the leader of the Spanish Communist party, has most frequently been singled out to receive the strongest criticism. In 1977, for instance, an article which appeared in the Soviet weekly *New Times* attacked Carrillo for "crude anti-Sovietism," "slanderous accusations" against Soviet policy, and for taking "unsavory positions."

From the attack on Carrillo, the article moved on to condemn the Eurocommunist movement as a whole. *New Times* called Eurocommunism an invention of "middle-class theorists" who refuse to recognize the leadership of the Soviet Union in party affairs. Later in 1977, another article in the Soviet journal *Problems of History of the Soviet Communist Party* took a second stab at Eurocommunism. This time, the writer condemned the ideas of "peaceful change" and "political pluralism." Violent revolution, he contended, is an essential part of Communist doctrine. The Eurocommunists delude themselves if they believe they can be voted into office. The time will come when they will have to take up arms against the middle class in order to destroy the old social system. Revolution and dictatorship are the only truly Communist ways to power.

The unspoken reason behind the Soviet attitude toward Eurocommunism is the fear that Eurocommunism could upset the balance of power in Europe and lead to a crisis between the United States and the Soviet Union. For several years, the USSR has carried on successful relationships with the governments of Italy, France, and Spain. If the Eurocommunists came to power, these relationships would be undermined and drastically altered. For that reason alone—to insure international stability and harmony—the Soviet Union has opposed the Eurocommunists and hopes they will never come to power.

The United States, too, opposes Eurocommunism for reasons of international stability and the preservation of the status quo. As mentioned earlier, three American Presidents—Nixon, Ford, and Carter—have declared themselves against

Communist participation in the governments of Western Europe. But perhaps the most articulate opponent of Eurocommunism among American statesmen has been Dr. Henry Kissinger, the former Secretary of State under Presidents Nixon and Ford. In June 1977, Dr. Kissinger addressed a conference on Eurocommunism held in Washington, D.C. The success of Eurocommunism, he warned, "would alter the prospects for security and progress for all free nations."

Why is Eurocommunism so dangerous? Because, Kissinger answered, the Eurocommunists could not be trusted to stand by their allegiance to democracy and their desire for political pluralism. Time and time again, he pointed out, Communists have claimed to accept freedom and diversity only to abandon these ideals once they seize power. Nor is there any reason to trust the Eurocommunists when they abandon such traditional Communist notions as the dictatorship of the proletariat. "One need not be a cynic," Kissinger concluded, "to wonder at the decision of the French Communists, traditionally perhaps the most Stalinist party in Europe, to renounce the Soviet concept of dictatorship of the proletariat without a single dissenting vote among 1,700 delegates, as they did at their party congress in February 1976, when all previous party congresses had endorsed the same dictatorship of the proletariat by a similar unanimous vote of 1,700 to nothing."

The Future of Eurocommunism. The dilemma of Eurocommunism, then, is to maintain its positions in spite of the large number of voters who regard it suspiciously and in spite of the opposition of the Soviet Union and the United States. It will be a difficult task and one requiring a great deal of patience and continued participation in the democratic system.

But before this book is brought to an end, let us speculate on what would happen if Eurocommunism were to prove successful. What would take place if Eurocommunists gained control of key Cabinet posts or if a Eurocommunist became a Premier or a Prime Minister? The answers, naturally, must vary from nation to nation, just as the Communist parties of each nation vary in background, platform, and degree of commitment to Eurocommunism.

In Italy, the success of Eurocommunism would not create a radical break with the Italian past because the Italian Communist party long ago began the process of expansion and development that has led to its present position. The one consistent thing that the PCI has promised Italian voters has been clean government, a government free of the corruption that has plagued the Christian Democrats. Great pressure would be exerted by the public on the Communists to keep that promise or face a loss of popular support. Most observers agree, however, that the temptations of office would prove too great. They point to several scandals that have already shaken the Communist party and argue that the Communists will prove as corrupt as the Christian Democrats once they assume power.

If victorious, the PCI would likewise face the problem of national unity. It would have to steer a course between right and left and not move too rapidly—or too slowly— toward social and economic reform. Like the Christian Democrat governments of recent years, a Communist government would probably be a minority government, one plagued by the constant need to search for partners to prop up its position and give it the extra votes required to control Parliament. The PCI would then most likely concentrate on building a large body of leftist support that would return the Communists to power in future elections.

In France, a victory for the Communists could well mean a complete break with some aspects of French tradition. The PCF, in its Common Platform with the Socialist party, plans a large number of nationalizations that would alter the basic character of the French economy. French communism is likewise deeply anti-American and anti-German and might demand an end to the defensive and economic alliances that have bound France to the United States and Germany for many years.

The only chance for PCF participation in the government at this time, however, is through its union with the Socialists, and the Socialists would work to mitigate the more extreme measures that might be advocated by some Communists. The basic problem of a Socialist and Communist coalition government would be the harmony and agreement of the two parties. If the Socialists and Communists could govern together without arguments and bitter quarrels, they could carry out a significant program of social and economic change.

The possibility of the Spanish Communist party gaining power through any means is extremely remote. For years to come, the PCE will be involved in building Spanish democracy and in striving for acceptance and respectability. Any hint that Spanish communism might play a part in national government would provoke a reaction on the part of the Spanish right, which remains strong and influential.

INDEX

ABOUT THE AUTHOR

Stephen Goode is a former member of the history faculty at Rutgers University. He holds degrees in history from Davidson College, the University of Virginia, and Rutgers. His master's thesis was on the Socialist and Communist revolutions in Hungary in 1918 and 1919, and his doctoral thesis was on the cultural and social crisis of Eastern Europe in the last half of the nineteenth century.

A free-lance writer with many fine books to his credit, Mr. Goode's most recent book for Franklin Watts was a study of the assassinations of John F. Kennedy, Martin Luther King, Jr., and Robert F. Kennedy, called *Assassination!*. Mr. Goode lives in Washington, D.C., where he can keep a close eye on the subjects nearest and dearest to him—government and politics.